WORLDS APART

~~~~~~~~~~~~~~~~~~

my personal life journey
through transcultural
poverty, privilege & passion

~~~~~~~

Mai Kim Le

Printed in the United States of America

ISBN-13: 978-1-954968-90-5

Waterside Productions
2055 Oxford Ave, Cardiff, CA 92007
www.waterside.com

Artwork Cover

Title: "Girl" by Ha Duong

Private collection, 2020

https://haduongart.com

Author Photograph

By Joe Lee © Mai Kim Le 2021

http://www.joeleefoto.com/

Dedication

~~~~~~~~~~~~~~~~~~~~~~~~~~~~

*Leah, this book was written
with you in my heart and mind!*

To Leah, Elan, and Ezra:

*For helping me grow and heal ...
for reminding me how life is so precious,
even my own. I may not say these words
often, but my love for each of you
has no bounds.*

*And to my husband and true life partner
through so many loving years,
untold passionate thanks.*
~~~~~~~~~~~~~~~~~~~~~~~~~~~~

"In true dialogue both sides are willing to change."

Thich Nhat Hanh

Foreword

~~~~~~~~~~~~~~~~~~~~~~

When Mai asked me to write this foreword to *Worlds Apart* I thought I knew where I would begin and what I would say. After all, we have a deep 21-year old friendship. She was my lifeline in grad school – we shared an apartment. She drove me to lectures in her Jeep. She took me home to Boston for a Vietnamese-American Thanksgiving. We went shopping and *oohed* and *aahed* in outlet malls together, and spent weekends in New York with her friends there. Most importantly, she introduced me to my future husband.

Mai still remains the person I can call at any time, even across 12-hour time differences. I've known many bits and pieces of her life journey as a refugee, her poverty-ridden childhood, her struggles during college. I know about her youthful crushes and her one true love. About her challenges in the workplace and with her children – the three beautiful ones she has and those who weren't meant to be. So yes, I thought I knew Mai very well. But then I read her *Worlds Apart* manuscript and realized just how much I didn't know.

Mai is that rare person who doesn't pretend to be more than she is – but who is actually so much more than meets the eye. She often talked with me about being a refugee, about living hand to mouth growing up, about her Vietnamese roots and her ever-evolving identity. I now realize that she had to dig very deep, and tell her story in all
~~~~~~~~~~~~~~~~~~~~~~

its unfiltered rawness, in order to bring who she is, and why she is, into sharp relief.

I realize I cannot do justice to Mai's story in this short forward. Her vivid and beautiful words come right from the heart, tumbling eagerly and bravely out into the world as she speaks. I know that she has often said she's not eloquent enough, not fluent enough, to express her deeper truths. But as this book clearly demonstrates, she both can and now has fully told her story with literary finesse – a story that mirrors America itself.

In essence this story is a tale of determination, of survival. It documents a life of many setbacks finally overcome, and some not yet conquered. Her account is at times a heartbreaking yet ultimately triumphant portrayal of the internal roiling of currents that shape who we are. And now she has created this work of literature that courageously bares her soul, come what may – and really, how brashly American is that! All I can say, to paraphrase Elena Ferrante, is: here is my brilliant, courageous friend.

Mehvesh Mumtaz Ahmed

TABLE OF CONTENTS

Preface

~~~~~~~~~~~~~~~~~~~~~~~~~~~~

This book strives to be an amalgamation of an action-adventure immigrant tale and a quite-complicated love story. It's a personal-growth journey through the challenges of war, poverty, discrimination, work and wealth. I've been wanting to write my personal story for many years, in the hope of speaking up and speaking out on issues that are rarely discussed – considered socially uncomfortable and often culturally unacceptable.

My daughter's struggles during COVID were the catalyst for me to embark on this project of penning my story. I very much wanted to speak to her at deep levels and show her what I went through. But unfortunately the experiences I've shared in this book, of struggling to break free from the anxieties and restrictions of my traditional upbringing, had hardened me – preventing me from openly expressing to my own daughter my buried feelings of love and understanding. Writing this book has softened my heart – and helped me to truly understand and hear her.

It's true that we don't fall far from the tree of our heritage. Despite my many efforts to parent differently than my cultural heritage, it took many failure as a person and a parent to embrace the transformation I've been trying to achieve. I still have difficulty communicating to my daughter in a way that connects us. This book is my attempt to personally heal, myself, and already in unanticipated ways writing it has helped to bring me closer to my daughter, siblings, friends and spouse.
~~~~~~~~~~~~~~~~~~~~~~~~~~~~

The actual day-to-day process of writing this book was one of the most challenging experiences I've ever known. I had no option but to approach this story with blunt openness. Sharing my deepest secrets and bringing skeletons out of the memory closet was very hard. Reliving the more intense moments of my life often left me in tears of both pain and joy. The difficult moments were tough to recall and work through – at times excruciating but also liberating, offering a much needed release.

On broader levels, through this book I want to break the traditional Vietnamese code of silence, and in doing so to amplify our shared Asian-American voice. In these current times raising our communal voice is more important than ever as we strive to bridge the cultural gaps that continue to keep us worlds apart.

Speaking up honestly, taking the road less traveled, is of course often met with challenges and conflicts we must face both within ourselves, and with our family and society. Ultimately I do believe that this process of honest and open discussion will help us gain a better understanding of one another – so that we can heal and grow as a compassionate world community.

My deepest hope in writing this book is that we all can learn to open up our hearts, eyes and ears as we discover that many of the so-called differences that hold us worlds apart are actually not that different. Our personal journeys are often very different – but our individual struggles so often induce shared unhealthy feelings of stress, anxiety, guilt, shame, hostility and despair. When we realize the universal similarities we all embody as human beings, we can perhaps learn to let go of feeling worlds apart and open our hearts and bridge our differences.

Mai Kim Le

PART ONE

~~~~~~~~~~~~~~~

Vietnam Escape
~~~~~~~~~~~~~~~

Chapter One

I've decided to tell my story from the very beginning, back in Vietnam, because part of what drives me today – how I behave and carry myself, how I raise my family, how I approach my career – was so deeply impacted by my first years of life.

I was born in 1978 on a riverbank in the Mekong Delta, up one of the minor tributaries of the 'mother of all rivers'. This was three years after the war ended. My father had fought in the war on the south side with the Americans, and then he came back to his home village and married my mom in 1977. He was Buddhist, a slender man of average height, with high cheekbones and wavy hair that resembled a 'fro if left long.

My mom was petit, around 5'4" with a heart-shape face that complemented my dad's more structured features. My father had to convert to Catholicism in order to marry her. Mom's family had been well-to-do in the region, but they'd lost everything during the two terrible decades of conflict.

Twenty years later, when I was in college, I went back to see the place where I was born. It's still just a muddy rural bank littered with ramshackle houseboats, way out in nowhere next to a very silty delta tributary. There's almost nothing there except for lush rice paddies and palm and coconut trees surrounded on all sides by water and jungle. So I guess I'm basically a jungle baby born on the river.

The impact of the war was absolutely devastating, leaving over three million people dead and a verdant, resource-rich country in abject poverty and total destruction. Those were, to say the least, really hard times – and after the war there was almost no food to eat, really nothing at all. My local village was just trying to survive while staying under the radar from the Viet Cong.

My father didn't want this life for his family – and besides, he was being hunted by the Viet Cong for his participation on the other side of the conflict. So he decided to risk everything in pursuit of stability and opportunity, since the outlook was bleak in post-war Vietnam. For more than a year my parents lived entirely off the grid in hiding on their houseboat. And that location would make it relatively easy to sail down the delta and out to sea, to make an escape.

My dad took the lead, secretly organizing an escape for a group of around forty people. He asked everyone in the group to pack and be ready for the day they would flee together. The time and location of the escape would only be known a few hours before departure, to reduce the risk of the plan leaking out to the Viet Cong. When that day came, my dad signaled to each family group where and when to meet – one o'clock in the morning about sixty miles down-river from our village.

Being knowledgeable about boats, my dad quietly took over a rickety fishing boat that would carry our group east and down the river, out onto the open sea and freedom. He made sure everything was in readiness, and then waited anxiously for everyone, including me and my mom, to arrive. I was just one year old at the time so of course I don't remember any of this, but I'm told that everyone was feeling naturally anxious.

Under the cover of darkness, my mom sailed with me, her uncle and his family downstream from our village as we'd planned. My parents decided to meet several hours earlier than the departure time. But at the designated departure time, with my father impatiently waiting for our arrival, we were still nowhere to be found. Dad had searched for us for 4-5 hours prior to departure with no luck. He knew far too well that the longer the boat waited around at the dock to depart, the higher the chance of being caught by the Viet Cong. Everyone else was already on board and my dad waited as long as he could – but then he had to take responsibility for everyone already present on the boat, and leave without his own family.

He's recently told me how agonizing that departure was for him, as the boat sped down stream toward the ocean … without me and my mom. But like I said, those were tough times, and my dad's anguish at having to leave behind his wife and child was overshadowed by his immediate job of keeping everyone on the boat alive and safe until they reached Thailand.

Before dawn they made it to open ocean in the Gulf of Thailand. The sea that day was calm and quiet – but for the escapees, the early morning was filled with many mixed emotions on the boat – sadness at leaving the homeland, relief at not having been caught, along with fatigue, hunger, excitement, and also lots of refugee hope. But back up-river at that same time, having been unavoidably delayed as a result of meandering to the wrong location in the dark, imagine how my mom felt when she got to the meeting point and found that my dad had left without us.

Meanwhile my dad piloted the escape boat toward Thailand as planned, running at high throttle for twelve hours – until a Viet Cong military boat came roaring up behind them and forced the boat to a halt. With machine guns aimed at him and his fellow boatmates, Dad was roughly arrested and then taken back upstream and thrown in jail in the nearby city of Rach Gia.

But – he managed to escape from prison just thirty minutes after being locked up. He saw a sudden chance to jump out of a second-floor window, and soon returned to his village to surprise me and my mom. Rumors had begun to spread that he'd purposefully deserted his family – but when he almost magically reappeared, the rumors were dispelled. His sharp fight-or-flight responses, fine-tuned by years of combat, had enabled him to succeed with his dangerous life-or-death decisions to slip out of jail.

Unfortunately, all our family funds had now been spent on the bungled sea escape, and the process of putting together another attempt from Vietnam was quite unthinkable without money for a boat and basic resources like gasoline and food. But then unexpectedly a year later, an opportunity arose for another escape attempt. The son of a former high-level South Vietnamese government official offered my dad a boat if he could again secretly plan and lead a group out of Vietnam.

This boat gave my dad a hopeful shot at another attempt to achieve something better than the local Vietnamese status quo – but this time he vowed not to take off unless we were with him at all times. This required him to find someone who could captain such a boat out on the open sea. Dad quietly found a sea fisherman skilled at navigating large bodies of water. I met this man later on when I was five, and heard his version of bravery, even heroically steering an old faded-grey wood boat down-river and out onto the Gulf of Thailand.

Dad made a few changes to his escape plan to make it more foolproof. Suspecting that the first attempt had been fouled because the authorities had heard about the plan, he now set up clandestine meetings to arrange access to the boat. And this time he was even more selective regarding who would be part of the small group to flee the country.

He decided that his younger sister and his brother, along with a few close childhood friends, would join him on this journey, as well as others he trusted who could afford to help pay for the boat and supplies. He and my mom didn't inform anyone outside the group that they were leaving Vietnam, except for my dad's parents. My mom's family didn't even know she had left. And everyone in the group knew that this journey could have three outcomes – freedom or prison or death.

Despite the questionable outcome, everyone who committed to flee was clearly willing to die for freedom. At the time it seems that both my parents had no fear of dying. When the day of the escape arrived my parents and I hid on a boat sailing down from the delta out to meet up with the larger boat. Even this first step of the escape was very hard to make as I was a colicky infant.

The reason I was crying so much was because I almost never had enough to eat. I was just bone and skin, with my mom struggling to nourish a one-year-old without adequate food, and also being pregnant again herself. Like I said, the local situation after the war was tough and starvation was the norm.

But we made it down to the main boat, and then managed to set off for Thailand around 11 PM that night. But the son of the government official didn't make it to the boat in time to flee with us. As before with me and my mom, it would have been too risky to wait around for him and risk the entire group getting caught.

We were crammed together on board with 36 other people including five young, skinny and scared children, me being the youngest. Soon we were hurrying down the river in the darkness, and then venturing out into the vast ocean facing the lurking possibility of large waves and sudden storms and everything that comes with being in such a precarious situation.

We continued to move through the darkness in silence except when I was crying. And welcome relief swept through the boat when dawn broke over the horizon of the sea and no Viet Cong boats were in sight. But I'm sure no one felt any peace of mind. The hearts and souls of the refugees were undoubtedly still filled with the anxiety of what might happen next. And then damn – shortly after dawn the fast boat of some dreaded Thai pirates, not Viet Cong, appeared on the horizon and chased after our boat.

Our old rusty engine did its very best – but we failed to escape the notorious grasp of Thai pirates. For a long time afterwards, when I would talk about Thai pirates, no one would quite believe me. But then when I was in grad school I met a man named Brian who'd been stationed in Vietnam with the State Department, and he said, "Yes, there were definitely Thai pirates."

These terrible sailor-scavengers attacked and pillaged our boat until nothing was left. They were utterly cruel – they even threw all our food and gasoline overboard and also raped every woman except for those who held young children. During the attack, Thai pirates, so I'm told, wanted to chop off both my ears with a machete because I was wearing gold-hoop earrings. At that time in Vietnam, it was a tradition to pierce a girl's ears at a young age, around the one-month birthday that was a major milestone – infant mortality was common then.

Also, back in Vietnam many people didn't believe in banks, so they used jewelry as their way of storing wealth. When making an escape, they could carry gold with them and later trade it in for money. Anyway, I'd had my ears pierced at one month and sported two small gold hoops, and those pirates wanted to chop off my ears to get the hoops. My mom says she begged and begged them for mercy while she also somehow managed to get the earrings off and hand them over to the pirates.

Perhaps because of all that, to this day I still celebrate my ears with a collection of piercings and earrings. People don't understand why I love wearing earrings so much – but it's because for me they have this special deeper meaning. I'm grateful to still have these ears! My grandmother back in Vietnam, even as poor as she was, used to ask people who were going to the U.S. to bring me gold earrings. This was her way of saying, here's a part of me, here's a little bit of savings for you – and if you're ever in a bad time, you can turn this gold into money to get by. So yes, jewelry has a really meaningful place in my heart.

So the pirates came aboard our rickety old boat and pillaged and raped – and then coldheartedly left us to starve and die out at sea. As you might imagine, after the pirates left us adrift to die, the boat was filled with pure fear of death and loss of hope. And my father felt the immense responsibility, as the leader of the group, to ensure that death wasn't imminent and that there was still a glimmer of hope.

He started ripping up pieces of wood from the boat and asking everyone to use them to paddle – but no one wanted to paddle, they had already given up hope. Some prayed, asking God for help. My father told them that God couldn't help them in this situation, only paddling could. Hope was lost.

My dad decided to change everyone's perspective. He believed that if he jumped into the ocean, everyone would paddle to him to make sure he doesn't drown or get swallowed by a shark. That is what he did and he swam as far away from the boat as possible, and everyone paddled as fast as possible to him. After the psychological exercise was met with success, my dad climbed back in and instructed everyone to paddle for as long as possible.

We remained at sea for many more hours until a packet of 555 cigarettes floated by. My dad told the crew that this is a good sign. It meant that someone was nearby. That persuaded some, but not all. Shortly after that, a piece of turd floated by. My dad rejoiced and so did others. That meant they were close to humans. Who knew that turd could bring so much hope? They continued to paddle and came across a piece of wood with nails. They knew they were close to land.

Nearly 24 hours after escaping Vietnam luck was with us, and a larger boat from Singapore came and rescued us. My father instructed everyone that children must be saved first, then women, and men last.

That all happened when I was around a year old. The one vivid memory from that escape that would play over and over in my mind later on was seeing and feeling someone lifting me up, and then someone else grabbing me – and at that moment I saw a small boat and a big boat next to each other. For the next several months in various refugee camps and through my early childhood, I kept experiencing that same memory, of being lifted up and then grabbed and taken by someone, I don't know who.

That same image replayed in my mind in my childhood whenever I closed my eyes for bed. It felt like a scene in a movie on rewind. With age, that memory faded, no longer appearing in my dreams. But I created in my youthful mind, from bits and pieces that I learned of from relatives, a dramatic story of our escape – with my dad as the hero, which he in fact was.

When you meet my dad today you'd never think this frail, chiseled cheek, curly hair Vietnamese man had planned and pulled off a dangerous escape for a whole group of family and friends. I no longer eulogize him for his bravery, but I do deeply respect and thank him for what he was able to do.

And so we ended up in a Thai refugee camp near Bangkok for two months. Those were very hard times and my parents to this day hate Thailand and hate Thai people. And, considering all that happened, I don't blame them, I understand where that hatred came from. In fact, they hate everything Thai so much that twenty years later, when I accepted a UNDP internship in Thailand, they refused to talk to me that summer.

While living in that Thai camp we often didn't have any food, my mom had to go out to Bangkok and beg for a bowl of rice, often with her carrying me. She begged and begged every day for a bowl of rice. She put all her humility aside and simply did it … because it was survival. That's probably why, even now, whenever I see someone on the street begging for money, I always try to give them something – because you never know what their situation is. As long as I give them even a little bit, I feel comfort in that.

After being in the Thai refugee camp for two months, we were transferred to Singapore for two weeks before ending up in a refugee camp in Galang Island in the Riau Archipelago of Indonesia where nearly 150,000 refugees passed through between 1979 and 1996. We were the first wave of refugees to go through Galang. My brother's name is the namesake of that place where he was born and where we were processed as refugees.

Inevitably we were exposed to all sorts of things like lice, hepatitis, and tuberculosis because we were packed like sardines sleeping on the floor on mats of some sort. It would look and feel terrible to the world, but it was refuge that so many risked their lives for. There was food (Spam and rice), tin roofs and four walls, water, and no Thai pirates. The necessities were taken care of, so anything more was icing on the cake.

We were finally interviewed there to see where we would go – to the U.S., Canada, France, Australia or whatnot. Because my father had fought on the U.S. side of the war, he had a bit of priority for the U.S. coupled with a church in Seattle offering to sponsor us. That's how we were able to fly away from Indonesia and hopefully to a much better future.

PART TWO

~~~~~~~~~~~~~~~

West Coast / Hard Landing
~~~~~~~~~~~~~~~

Chapter Two

~~~~~~~~~~~~~~~~~~~~~~~~~~

I was around three when we landed in America, the five of us: me, my mom and dad, my uncle in his teens, and my infant brother. We landed with nothing at all except one little green bag. That's all we had, but it was important because that green bag had all our paperwork, immunizations, and documents that we'd received thus far. My mom still has that bag – she cherishes it and tries to preserve it as much as possible. I remember as a child going through that bag in the middle of the night when my parents were asleep, to see what was in it. I remember being five or six when I was doing that.

So we made it to this utterly foreign place called Seattle. We didn't speak any English at all, any of us, except maybe a few slang words with thick Vietnamese accents. But we were thankful – this new place on this Earth was our entry point, our crash landing into a dream called America.

That dream dropped us into one of the roughest neighborhoods of Seattle, in one of the subsidized government projects. It was rough but on the bright side, there weren't any Viet Cong in the woods, and there was almost always something for us to eat if we worked really hard all the time.

When I go back to Seattle these days and I tell people I lived in White Center and on Rainier Avenue, they are shocked and say 'no way you lived there, that's the hood.' But I tell them that back
~~~~~~~~~~~~~~~~~~~~~~~~~~

then, the hood was just reality, it made up a large part of my life in America. Before I made it into a college back east, rough poor neighborhoods were all I knew. It was my life from the time I was three until I was eighteen – and before I was twelve, things had been a thousand times rougher. In comparison my world in these enclaves of socio-economically depressed neighborhoods was good. It was all I knew. It was a crazy wild alive place, I was alive in the midst of it.

But weather-wise and culture-wise, in comparison with Vietnam, Seattle was not at all easy for my parents and uncle. Coming from a tropical place to a place that was dreary, rainy, cold and punkish – it was definitely a culture shock. I remember a lot of mohawks and cloudy days. When the sun graced the Seattle skyline with some drizzles, a rainbow appeared and always brought a smile to my face until I was brought back to reality. This was in the '80s and punk was a movement back then. I remember being fascinated with all of this, not feeling any fear at all.

But my parents felt very uncomfortable, to say the least, trying to live in this alternate culture. Imagine not being able to speak any English but having to go out on the streets, often at night, in a Seattle hood compounded by a seemingly-hostile punk fashion that appeared seriously scary. It's an understatement to say that my mom and dad didn't appreciate this bizarre American street culture. There was nothing wrong with punk culture, but we had a few bad encounters with punks.

The only thing on their minds, back then and for many years to come in America, was survival. "Let's just manage to eat and have a roof over our heads" – that was my dad's motto. So every day they went out and earned whatever they could by doing whatever needed doing, cleaning and sewing and serving and so forth. They were grateful for any money they could bring home to sustain us.

Looking back, all I can say is that it was really tough but I didn't think it was tough. And we all agreed that living here in our tiny apartment that we shared with another Vietnamese family was definitely better than life had been living back in Vietnam. And the community we lived in, well, this was just where we were – it was just what life had brought us.

When I took my own children back recently to show them where I'd lived as a little kid, they seemed unfazed and uninterested, even though the area has been gentrified a bit since then. What I remember is that, honestly, I thought our new world was pretty cool, being way over here in Seattle, in America the land of vast opportunities and fanciful dreams. I was just a few years old when we arrived, and I'm certain I had a much easier time with it all than my parents did.

On top of working all the time at menial jobs, mom and dad also tried to learn English at a local community college. This challenge was very hard for them, and it took quite a lot of time. Meanwhile my dad definitely felt non-stop stress, working so hard to get enough money to pay for a place to live – and all the while being surrounded and sometimes harassed by tough and seemingly-uncaring people. They were after all complete strangers to him, and sometimes downright violent.

As we would learn from my dad's medical difficulties while in Seattle, this same man who had so bravely masterminded his family's escape out of his own country's ongoing war zone had come out of that war with a terrible case of PTSD.

Life continued to be very difficult for my dad in Seattle, given the physical, emotional, and financial stress. He did sometimes seem to be temporarily in shock about everything going on around him – he just didn't know how to cope with this strange and at times hostile new world he'd brought his family into. I raised this Seattle period of our lives in conversation a few years ago – but I shouldn't have. It again brought up painful memories that seemed for him much more traumatic than the impulsive act of jumping from the second floor of that prison. I watched as tears started streaming down his chiseled cheeks, like the constant flow of rain in Seattle.

But during those early American years, my dad mostly succeeded in suppressing all of those agonizing feelings. Actually, he and my mom didn't have any free time at all to think about the past or deal with their feelings. They both had to let go at least superficially because our life was so tenuous in Seattle with both of them often off working multiple jobs every day.

Only when all four of his children had left the house and gone off to college or wherever, sometimes all his past memories would come back to haunt him with a vengeance.

While I was growing up, I often felt like my dad actually hated me. He was so sweet to his other kids – but I was the eldest and I guess I symbolized something to him that the others didn't. I'd been born at a time when it was really hard, right after the war, to raise a family. And my colicky crying presence had made it extra hard for them to escape. Honestly, I don't blame him for his feelings. I can't imagine trying to flee a toxic country with a half-starved crying child.

But still I carried very hurt buried feelings in my heart because my parents never said 'I love you' to me. I would learn many years later, in grad school, that in contrast to American families, Asian parents traditionally don't say 'I love you' to their children. Instead they show their love in other ways, like getting them good educations, a safe neighborhood, and cooking tasty food for them.

For instance I once went to Senegal for research and stayed in a village where I caught some very nasty parasites. I was quite sick and lost a lot of weight, I was barely able to move for weeks – and my parents drove many hours to make me some healthy soup, only to drive back home to their jobs after cooking for me. That episode was when I finally realized how they convey their love – not through words but through action. It's just somehow too hard or unnatural for them to say 'I love you'.

Unfortunately that trait seems to have been passed down to me. I still have a hard time saying those words to my children and husband. Finally I went into therapy to learn how to better express my heart feelings – but still it doesn't feel natural, I'll say the words but it's not quite real. I will do everything and anything for anyone close to me, pull all-nighters, drive hours to do something for my kids or friends, take out loans to help pay college bills for my siblings and so on. And I now realize that this behavior pattern is similar to my parents, particularly my dad. I'll go beyond my means to help people – but I cannot say 'I love you' as easily as most people in America do.

And it's apparently the same with many refugees when asked to talk about past negative experiences in the old country. I once helped a Harvard grad student with her research on Vietnamese immigrant communities, and found out that most of them don't want to talk about their experiences back home, bad or good. They want to just forever put it all behind them, close it up, lock the box, throw away the key – and move forward into their new life. They try to forgive and forget, which often continues to be their model throughout life, even when people have really hurt them.

So, yeah – Seattle. I loved being a tiny imported part of that city even though my parents didn't. I remember going around and feeling like, wow, there are so many beautiful rainbows in the sky here, and it's always cool and green. The place still holds so many meaningful flashbacks – and our family struggle for survival felt entirely normal, I just assumed that's the way people live in America.

But I do hate Halloween because of Seattle. That's the one American holiday I despise. I remember when I was in kindergarten and my parents didn't even know what Halloween was. The older kids I knew in my neighborhood were like, 'let's go trick-or-treating, we'll take Mai with us.'

It seems that my parents felt comfortable sending me out with these older kids – but for me it was scary, so dark and chilly that night, and I could still barely speak any English. I had no idea what was going on but I was like, okay, I'll follow you guys. And at first it was all okay, I just opened my bag when we knocked on a door and people would throw candy in my bag and that was pretty fabulous.

But then all of a sudden there came a group of older punks with mohawks and they started chasing us. The kids that I was with panicked and took off running away – and I ended up the only one left behind. I was scared to death, running from the punks until I was out of breath and finally, tripping on some uneven sidewalk, plopped face-down on the ground.

I was beyond scared. I remember the first thought that raced through my mind was that I was going to die. But they just grabbed my candy and ran away. And then there I was, all alone in a dark unknown street, lost with no idea how to get home. I don't remember what happened but somehow someone must have helped me – my mind's still a blank about that trip home.

I swore after that trauma that I'd never go out on Halloween again. I remember going home that night in Seattle and dreaming of doing kung fu on these punk kids who stole my candy. I'd been watching Bruce Lee movies back then … but yeah, my worst memory of Seattle is about Halloween. Later as a parent, I'd be pushed into participating in Halloween activities because of my kids – but I can care less for the holiday.

Chapter Three

~~~~~~~~~~~~~~~~~~~~~~~~~~~~~

Then at some point a few years later, my parents decided to leave Seattle. They couldn't handle the weather, there was often no work for them – and they'd heard about a wonderful community way down in Southern California where a lot of Vietnamese people had recently settled. They'd also heard that the weather was much warmer and nicer.

So right after I completed first grade, we packed our bags and loaded up our old station wagon and all of us, including my uncle, my parents, my brother, and my sister who'd recently been born in Seattle – we took off headed south. I remember there were four of us in the back, and my uncle and dad up front. It was a long drive, over a thousand miles – just another Vietnamese family adventure as we headed off again into the great American unknown.

When we got into California, driving down the Pacific Coast Highway Route 1 just south of San Francisco, I recall looking down and seeing big scary cliffs on our right side. Without thinking I made a quick move, reaching for something from my uncle on the other side of the car – and somehow the car swerved and we almost drove off the cliff. We all thought we were going to plunge into the ocean and die – and I got blamed for the incident. My dad screamed at me but I was a very quiet kid, I just bowed my head to conceal any tears.
~~~~~~~~~~~~~~~~~~~~~~~~~~~~~

Later on, I kept recalling this incident and the trip down to Los Angeles, and when I turned forty I told my husband I didn't want a party. Instead, I wanted to go out west to Big Sur and drive down Route 1 again, as a way to make closure. And oh my gosh, it was so beautiful and mesmerizing seeing it the second time, this time as an adult. The first time driving down had at times been so traumatic.

But finally we made it down to Anaheim. My parents found an apartment that we ended up sharing with another family. It was a small place in a large complex of Mexicans, Vietnamese, and Cambodians, located across from the Loara Elementary School. The housing complex even had a pool surrounded by tropical palm trees. The pool looked like so much fun but we could never go in. My parents were deathly afraid of water – perhaps because of their near-death experience when leaving the Mekong Delta in Vietnam. They kept us away from water and they didn't let us learn how to swim. They said it was safer just to stay away.

But every day when they went to work, picking strawberries in the field or doing some other menial work like sewing at a garment factory, whatever they could find – they always left us alone to watch out for ourselves. There was no alternative to that. And as the eldest, even when I was just six years old I was supposed to watch my three-year-old sister and four-year-old brother.

And sure enough, one day for some reason we decided to go to the pool – and my little sister decided to jump right into the water. She very nearly drowned. Someone saw what was happening and had to jump in to save her. My parents didn't learn that this had happened until much later – and when I finally mentioned it to them, about a decade ago, they just didn't believe me.

Regardless of such incidents, I loved California. I loved hearing the nightly fireworks coming from nearby Disneyland, and I loved the balmy weather with the sun caressing my skin nearly every day of the year. But school was very hard because I could still barely read or write or speak English. I attended our neighborhood elementary school but I couldn't understand much of what the teachers were talking about.

However, we sang beautiful songs before class started each morning, like *America the Beautiful* and *It's a Small World* and some others, and of course we always devotedly said our American pledge of allegiance to the flag. I hardly understood what the big patriotic words meant, but I could recite them quite proudly in my thick Vietnamese accent.

During our years in SoCal, I still had almost no realization of just how poor we were. I remember once when we went to a grocery store, I was so hungry I saw a nut on the floor and picked it up and was about to put it in my mouth – but my mom slapped it out of my hand. I then saw a maggot come out of it, but I didn't care. I just wanted food.

For the very longest time, until college, I grew up with little food to eat on a daily basis, so food itself has always been very important to me. The creation of dishes and the gathering of family and friends around those dishes has a very special meaning. I explore food the way the late Anthony Bourdain did in his *Parts Unknow*n TV series, I enjoy a permanent love affair with food.

My mom has sometimes called me *Parts Unknown* due to my similar relationship with food that Bourdain expressed in his TV programs. When the Bourdain episode in Hanoi aired, we were all deeply touched and excited for that passionate open-hearted presentation of the Vietnamese people on American television. I've watched and rewatched that hour-long ode to Vietnam, which warms my heart each time.

In case you haven't seen that episode ("Hanoi" Season 8, Episode 1) it includes half an hour with a surprise guest who was none other than Barack Obama. He had come to Hanoi as a strong gesture of compassion and solidarity with the Vietnamese people to help heal the lingering wounds caused by the Vietnam War. I'll always be deeply thankful to Obama and Bourdain for that *bun cha* noodle meal they shared in Hanoi. They talked so honestly and eloquently about forgiveness, healing, and turning enemies into friends. Their conversation over a traditional Viet meal helped bring our 'worlds apart' cultures closer.

As I mentioned before, in general, food is love in my family and many Vietnamese families. When my parents or relatives prepare a meal, or ask if I've eaten ("Con, ăn rồi chưa?"), it's their way of showing they care. What's that saying: 'The way to a man's heart is through his stomach'? Male or female, it's the same. And Vietnamese people love to gather together around wonderful dishes, as Bourdain so beautifully portrayed in his Hanoi episode. Bourdain's overt love of Vietnamese cuisine definitely helped break the stigma regarding anything Viet as well as elevated Vietnamese food to the American table.

Food is definitely central in my life – but like I mentioned, back in my childhood in Seattle and Los Angeles we often simply couldn't afford it. My parents cooked whatever they could get their hands on, and we rationed that supply. We would usually have just a small bowl of rice and a bit of meat for dinner – and those inexpensive childhood meals are still my comfort foods: crispy Spam and rice; sardines in chili and tomato sauce; caramelized salty pork and rice with bananas or cucumbers. I always felt hungry – and then as a teenager when things were better for my family financially, I would still over-eat when we were invited somewhere.

People who saw me, like at church, always thought I had parasites because I was skin and bones. I was also quite tall for my age, so people called me a flamingo. They also used to comment on how ugly I was because I had a big nose compared with other Vietnamese girls, and big dark goggle eyes – but I didn't say anything. I was always quiet because my parents taught me to be obedient and deferential to everyone, especially my elders, regardless of what they said or how they said it.

Because I was so quiet, people also thought I was not very bright – and for years I just went along with that also. Even when I started my freshman year in high school, I remember sitting next to a classmate who mentioned the word valedictorian. I asked her, "What is a valedictorian?" and she did not elaborate and I went on not knowing what that word meant.

As a child I didn't ever say much, I just kept to myself. I didn't talk about people. I went along with the flow – and no one thought of me as clever, smart, or witty. When I finally started opening up my shell and exploring the world, my parents were surprised that I knew so much about so many topics. For example, when I was twelve I helped my parents close on their first house. I translated things for them, and because they were off working so much I took care of my siblings' needs and their problems, and of course always helped to manage the house.

While I was in high school my parents began to make comments about how there was something different about me, but they didn't know what. I guess I still don't know what makes me different. I'm just quirky, and from an early age I've always worked very hard. I wasn't seen as real smart but I seemed to succeed by trying and trying and never giving up. I'm internally driven, people would say – I simply cannot sit still nor ease up and just do nothing for a while. I feel that if I'm not doing anything then I'm a lazy person and have no worth.

As a result of my formative years in grammar school in California, I must admit that I still feel like I'm a California girl at heart. Whenever I revisit California I somehow feel set free again, I feel like no one is judging me. When I went back to Big Sur on my fortieth birthday, I felt as if all the pressures and worries and all my past were suddenly, almost miraculously gone.

For me there's something quite ephemeral about California and Seattle and the whole West Coast that makes me feel a most wonderful liberation. And every now and then I need to go back. Who knows why – I just need to tap into that fresh sense of pure freedom again. Some friends say it's just because Los Angeles is so sunny and whatever – but it's deeper than that.

Another city that makes me feel this way is Paris. I studied abroad in Paris for six months when I was twenty and the first two months, oh my god, they were my worst time ever. I thought that the French people were rude and mean, and I became so terribly lonely – I was an absolute outsider. But I decided to make the best of Paris anyway, so I scheduled all my courses to take place on Mondays and Tuesdays so that I'd have five-day weekends. Also the professors gave out their assignments for the whole semester, so I completed all my assignments in the first month and then had loads of time free to myself.

And what did I do in Paris? I sat on benches in every little corner of the city, even the more dangerous neighborhoods – and I just … observed. This in itself was a major shift for me, because always before, like I said, I was a doer, not a witness to the life around me. But somehow I emerged from my feeling of acute loneliness into an almost delicious state of highly- enjoyable aloneness. And through doing this passive silent observing, day after day, my abundance of quiet total-retreat time allowed me to also go deeper inside my own self … and step by step, through some sort of natural spontaneous awakening process, I was able to find myself.

Perhaps that's why I love Paris so much. I discovered myself from the inside-out there. And maybe it was the same in Seattle, Big Sur, Anaheim – these are places that make me feel like I'm not tied to anyone or anything. I feel like I have no burdens. All the weight that's usually heavy on my shoulders, which has been there since almost the beginning of my life, is being magically lifted.

In Anaheim I remember being in second grade one day and getting a scoop of ice cream – and feeling like this was the most important wonderful thing possible. I'd barely had anything to eat that day, and now I was getting to taste this amazingly sweet delight. My mom had given me 25 cents and I'd also earned 25 cents by plucking my Cambodian neighbor's graying hair. That's how I earned my ice cream epiphany.

California is known as an entrepreneurial haven where people can leap from obscurity into financial success. As I mentioned, my mom was often doing sewing, making a lot of garments for small companies. One day my parents decided to open up a garment factory of their own, just a little shop. They were soon working day and night to succeed with their tiny business – one shirt would bring 10 cents, a collared shirt might bring 25 cents.

I of course was expected to help out, even at my young age. Whenever someone they hired screwed up, I knew how to remove the threads so that they could resew it. But soon it turned out that the business wasn't working out – they just couldn't make enough money to cover the costs of everything in the shop and also afford food and essential things for us. They were losing so much money, and they owed so much to everyone.

So they decided it was a hopeless venture, and that it was time for our family to leave California. They'd heard that there were plenty of good jobs in the textile mills in Massachusetts. And we had relatives there who said Boston was a place where Vietnamese could have more consistent financial stability. So – right in the middle of my fourth grade, my father went east to check it out, and when he came home he told us we were moving – we would fly east across all of America to Boston where we'd live in a city called Worcester where there was a sizeable Vietnamese community.

When we flew into Boston a few weeks later I looked down and saw that there was snow on the ground and no leaves on most of the trees. Compared to California, Boston seemed gray and flat and old. And when we left the airport for Worcester everyone we saw on the streets were bundled up against the cold, reminding me of movies about Russia and Siberia.

It was indeed very cold and as we drove west for fifty miles to Worcester, most of the buildings looked run down and drab. Why does everything look so dirty here, I was thinking to myself, but I never said anything. I didn't yet appreciate that this was a much older culture than out west, and that these drab stone buildings were 'historical'.

We settled into Worcester on the third floor of a three-decker low-rent building where my mom's uncle lived on the second floor. Some other Vietnamese family lived on the first floor, and as usual, we shared our apartment with another family – we were constantly sharing. I was eight then, and I really hated being in New England. I loved California and didn't understand why we were here.

To add to the situation, I was surrounded by my mom's relatives who had come to America several years after we had. My great uncle who lived on the second floor was the same uncle who got lost with me, my mom, and his family in the middle of the night trying to reach my dad on the first escape boat. His wife started telling me stories about how my dad had left me and my mom during that first escape attempt – left us for another woman.

When I tried to verify this story, I found thankfully that none of it was true. The truth was that these relatives were still very angry at my dad because to be safe, and for other complex reasons, he hadn't invited them to take part in the second escape plans. Therefore they'd had to wait several years before escaping to America. They still held that grudge against my dad – and I guess because I was his eldest child and looked like him and walked like him, they also didn't like me.

I would later find out that I had in fact almost been left behind when my parents escaped the second time. But the real reason I had almost been left in Vietnam wasn't because of my father, it had been because his mother, my grandmother, was fervently begging him not to take me on the long journey – she was afraid that in my weak condition, I would never survive the sea or the travel. I was her first granddaughter and she didn't want to see me gone.

My grandmother on my father's side passed away many years ago. She was a remarkable woman living in the Buddhist tradition (different from my mom's family who were devout Catholics). She made a promise to herself that if we all made it safely to America, she would devote her life to Buddhism – separate herself from my grandfather, live a celibate life and just pray every day.

And so – when she got that first letter from my father that they were now safe in America, she immediately did as she'd promised herself. She devoted her life totally to Buddhism. My grandfather would remain with her in their house, but they would no longer live as man and wife, they would just be good friends sharing the same house – which they did for all those following years.

I finally managed to go back to Vietnam to visit her for the first time in 1998, when I was in college. The American government had lifted the embargo on Vietnam travel for Americans two years prior. And before that year I couldn't have traveled anywhere abroad anyway, because I still didn't have U.S. citizenship. Even though my parents had received their citizenship years before, somehow my application had gotten lost in a forgotten pile of government paperwork. I should have received my passport and so forth automatically because of my parents, but something had gone wrong.

As a teenager I'd tried hard several times to reach out to the government officials but I'd never heard back from them, the system at that time was apparently so backlogged. Citizenship was important to have, it was an ultimate goal for many of us – and ultimately good luck was with me. I happened to have a friend in college named James. His uncle was a congressman from Maine. I told James about my situation and he said he'd talk to his uncle. Literally in just weeks I received an invitation to come to Boston and get sworn in along with my brother.

There wasn't any formal ceremony. It was in an office at the Tip O'Neil building. My brother and I took the train into Boston and then treaded through a nasty blizzard. Finally we were taken into someone's office where an official performed the simple ceremony and voilà – we had our citizenship papers! My parents were blown away. They were, like, is this how America works?

I especially wanted that U.S. passport so that I could go back to Vietnam, and once I had it I did just that. I chose to go back with my mom – and when arriving, I found Vietnam to be very raw and vibrantly alive. I remember we had to get off the plane out in the middle of a runway that back then was just dirt. Then we took a bus that rambled off through the middle of the night for over six hours, through dark villages and across rivers on little dinky ferries, until we eventually made it to my paternal grandparents' humble home on the delta.

When I saw my grandmother for the first time I wanted to go hug her – but no, you don't hug each other in traditional families in Vietnam. You don't do any of that. Instead I had to reverently bow. I saw there were tears in her eyes, I knew she wanted to hug and touch me. But she held herself back, so I did too. I bowed to her and she walked away, silently crying.

I quickly began to see how my grandmother and grandfather lived – it was quite interesting, they would go around mumbling things about each other under their breath. They were almost constantly at odds with each other, which made the home's atmosphere a bit emotionally polluted. And also there was the sanitation situation.

My grandmother seemed to assume that since I was born here on the delta, I would be able to handle their water and their food. I said yeah, sure, no problem. I was so very respectful, I would do whatever they asked me to do. I didn't want to hurt anyone's feelings or appear to be rude or judgy.

They were actually living right on the Mekong River. Half the house was out on the water, and the bathroom had just a hole in the floor. You'd poop and it went right down into the river. When I arrived I went to the bathroom and did my thing, and when I came out my grandma said, "Let me make you some coffee." And she took a bucket of water from the same place where I just went to the bathroom.

I was silently dying inside, thinking about drinking my own pee and poop. But I said nothing and she proceeded to make coffee for me – and oh wow, everything I ingested and drank those first days made me so sick for a very long time – and my grandpa and grandma got into a fight about it. My grandfather yelled at her: "It's all your fault, lady!" And she retorted: "Well she was born here, she should have a strong stomach." Their bickering was just unbearable at times, but I also felt the love, and their pleasure that I was visiting them.

PART THREE

~~~~~~~~~~~~~~~

Lawrence Awakening
~~~~~~~~~~~~~~~

Chapter Four

Anyway, back to our move from Orange County to Boston. I was just miserable – I hated it. We were surrounded by Vietnamese refugees who talked way too much gossip and were continually commenting on how quiet I was, how ugly I looked, and how stupid I must be if I couldn't speak English after all these years.

And it was true – I had already been in the U.S. from preschool to fourth grade and I still couldn't speak much English, or read in any language. That was partly because I'd been in ESL (English as a Second Language) classes in SoCal which had been taught in Vietnamese – and also, we had moved around a lot. In California, we'd lived in Anaheim, Fullerton and Santa Ana.

All my ESL classes had been taught by Vietnamese teachers, so I hadn't needed to speak English. My only classes in English had been in math which was quite easy for me to learn. When my teachers gave math tests, I just saw numbers – and I understood numbers. I was really good at math, but I couldn't read or write or do anything else. My parents never cared about my grades. They just cared that we made it through the day unharmed and with adequate food and shelter.

Speaking of making it through the day, one of the other reasons we moved to the East Coast was because there were so many 'home raids' happening in our California neighborhoods by various local gangs. My parents became more and more afraid that

I might even be pulled into joining one of those gangs, even at my young age.

We were rightfully scared because people would be murdered during home raids. I remember hearing at church about a girl who brought home her boyfriend and his gang raided the house and killed the parents. So home raids were on our minds often in California. We were always locking our doors and windows – my father and uncle would constantly double check, and they wouldn't even let us go near the door if someone knocked.

We were just very scared of the world outside our door – and to this day I'm constantly going around before bedtime making sure all the doors are secured. My friends sometimes make fun of my seeming paranoia, they say: "You know you live in a pretty decent area." But because I grew up in some really very rough neighborhoods where we definitely had to lock our doors, that habit continues.

My parents always wanted a better opportunity for us, and they heard that there were better schools on the East Coast. They didn't know then that those good schools were only in certain communities. They mainly just wanted to be on the East Coast, far away from California gangs. They also naturally wanted to have a better income of some sort. And so … we came east.

Luckily the school my great uncle put me in happened to be actually pretty good, it's called the Tatnuck School in Worcester. The teachers quickly realized that I didn't have the level of reading and writing that I should have at that grade – and thankfully they were very helpful, they focused on teaching me how to read. By fifth grade I was able to actually read a simple book. Whether I understood the meaning or not was another story. Being able to string the words together was important enough to me.

But my parents didn't care, all they hoped for was that I would be able to make enough money when I grew up to keep food on the table and a roof over my head. My mom told me that, back then, she never thought we would ever become part of this strange new American society. It was beyond their understanding that we might someday integrate and assimilate.

Even now, seeing me where I am and seeing my siblings also succeeding, my parents don't quite know how to grasp it all, they don't know what to think of us. And they sometimes feel uncomfortable with how we've been assimilated into this new society. They feel proud, but they don't know how to embrace what we've become. Sometimes I take them along to local social gatherings, for instance I took them to a pitch contest where they were surrounded by people – and they didn't know what to say or do, so they just remained quiet.

During our first years in Massachusetts, I went to school but I also continued taking care of my siblings while my parents worked in purse factories, toy factories, whatever jobs they could find. Then by a lucky twist of fate someone suggested to my mom that she take the U.S. Postal Service exam. We had no idea what that was – but she had by this time managed to learn how to read and write some English, mostly through her jobs, and now she began studying day and night for this test.

When she took the exam she actually scored very well, and I think that was one of the proudest moments my parents had ever enjoyed in America. She was accepted for immediate Post Office employment, and received two placements – one in Shrewsbury, the other in Lawrence. Shrewsbury was a wealthier community and it was predominantly Caucasian, whereas Lawrence was and still is a culturally diverse inner city that is often stigmatized as a real rough place.

My parents decided on Lawrence, a run-down city with old red-brick mills and a river running through it, because there was a Vietnamese community there, and they felt more comfortable in that environment than in an all-white town. Also my father's childhood friend and boatmate lived in Lawrence. Shrewsbury would have better schools, but they didn't feel like they could fit in. Feeling out of place for them was even harder than enduring hunger.

So we left Worcester and moved to Lawrence, which is thirty miles north of Boston – and my mom started working at the post office delivering mail. They were so happy, it was the first time in their lives that they had a stable income. We lived on the first floor of a bright green triple decker off the main street, Broadway. I don't remember how much she was making but it was pretty decent, way higher than what they both could make working in garment factories. And having a guaranteed paycheck every week – that was a primary fulfillment of their refugee dream.

My father also found work at several different local companies, and they saved and saved until they could buy their own home, a single-family split-entry black house in Lawrence. It wasn't much but it was everything to them. To this day they won't sell it. And I loved living in Lawrence – finally I felt like I belonged and was accepted just as I was. I made some good friends there who were real community people, and very supportive. Well, actually my first year in Lawrence wasn't so bright because I was placed in the Bruce School in North Lawrence, and I was the only Asian student there – it was mostly Hispanic.

I had to take a bus to school and it was scary, I was teased a lot. Kids would climb on the bus and call me 'la china' and other names. I never said anything back even though they would bully me. Those kids were tough and street smart and it was all just really overwhelming for me. I'd get on the bus and just look down at the floor, stick to myself and not look at anyone – because you can look at someone the wrong way and get hurt.

This was in sixth grade, I'd finished fifth grade in Worcester, then we moved. But it was so bad at that school. For instance I got my period that year, at a young age, and when I'd go to the bathroom a group of girls would climb up and look at me over the stall while I changed my pad, then run off to tell everyone. It was terrible. I was totally scared to go to school. Each day was a torture – I definitely stood out like a sore thumb as the only 'china'.

But then things began to change, because I started to grasp the whole idea of learning. It was a new exciting world for me. I also learned how to rap with a couple of the girls, I remember rapping in front of the school, something about reaching for the stars. And around that time I started to speak out more, to use my English more often. My grammar wasn't perfect but I was able to get by.

And yeah, in junior high school I also learned a lot of street slang and some Spanish. I could tell people 'look' (mírate) and 'shut up' (cállate). I picked up cursing habits like 'puta' – and of course all the English swear words. When I go back to Lawrence even now, I can slip into speaking again like a local, I can fit in and make people feel comfortable around me. That sense of belonging to a community, of fitting in, meant so very much to me!

After sixth grade I changed schools and attended a junior high school. It was called Robert Frost School because he'd grown up in Lawrence. The school was in South Lawrence which was a little bit more diverse, with some Caucasians and other ethnic groups along with Hispanics. I started seventh grade at Robert Frost and very soon came under the influence of an amazing teacher. She was from a very large Irish family and had lived through World War II.

In the first few weeks of her English class, she introduced us to books like *Jane Eyre* by Charlotte Bronte. I'd just learned how to read, and that book struck me so deeply, I identified with the main character with her strong values and determination to live by her principles in all her struggles. As I started reading the great European novels, I fell in love with reading.

I soon discovered that I really enjoyed learning about all sorts of things. I had just started to successfully string words together into sentences – and suddenly here were entire stories unfolding. I felt amazed by the whole world of words and ideas and the entire literary and scientific universe that my schooling opened up for me. Sometimes I couldn't comprehend what I was reading but that didn't matter – I understood enough to get the general idea of the story.

And that was just the start of it. In seventh grade, I began to really seriously study and learn many topics. What a world out there to discover! I think my romantic streak began to develop at that time also, around puberty, with my young dreams becoming filled by brave handsome characters and such strong romantic actors.

I also started to explore other activities, like high jump and long-distance running. And – I really wanted to act! Our school was putting on our local version of *The Outsiders* and I wanted intensely to be in that play. I liked acting because I could first go off and memorize the lines, and then speak confidently in full sentences and paragraphs, just like the Pledge of Allegiance back when I was in SoCal. I loved acting because I could become a character and express ideas and feelings that I'd suppressed all my life up until then.

But beyond memorized lines, I could still barely speak English. I remember in eighth grade during field day I said, "The grasses is green." The person I was talking to laughed at my terrible grammar and I was so embarrassed that after that experience, I told myself never to speak until I was sure my grammar was correct. I'd memorize my words and only then risk saying them. Of course that wasn't the best approach to learning how to communicate – but that's what I did.

It was easy for me to memorize lines and then repeat them. I did get some roles to play in school drama, and I felt freed on stage to act out all sorts of attitudes and perspectives that I would never be allowed to express in real life situations. At some level I guess I found my true strong voice through acting. My parents expected me to always be quiet and reticent and reserved, to just say yes and respect everyone and everything – and never cause any trouble. But on stage I could act out all I wanted.

But there was a problem – my parents were still working long hours and they needed me as their eldest child to regularly take care of my three younger siblings. This meant that I couldn't stay after school to rehearse, even if I got a part to play. So I tried to compromise and for instance in *The Outsiders* took one of the smaller parts – but it was at least one step into acting, and it didn't require staying after school a lot.

Then I got out of junior high and went into high school. Somehow the new campus and everything wasn't daunting or anything – I just thought it was another day at school. But I was exposed to a lot of new classes and things to learn in that new school, things that truly opened up my world. I remember receiving an algebra book and immediately thinking, wow, I love this! I started doing the algebra curriculum ahead of the class assignments, and quickly went through the whole book. I did the same with my chemistry book – I became totally immersed in learning.

I didn't tell my parents about my sudden fascination with math and science, I just went on my way, and the same thing happened with every new course. I felt like I was living in a dream, learning things that I'd never had an opportunity to delve into or even imagine before. My school was considered the roughest shittiest high school in the area and the state (the school lost its accreditation a year after I graduated) – but still I learned so much, and thought that my school was the best school … at least for me.

In reflection, this was the first place where I actually learned about the process of education. Most of the teachers really cared about me, cared about the growth of their students – yeah, it was a tough school, people could be mean and there were fights and gunshots. You name it, we had it all. One year on the first day of cross-country, we had to run a ten-miler to get our bodies used to long runs. As we went running through Lawrence I saw someone in the act of stealing a car right next to us – but I was used to that.

Most important, by the time I graduated I felt like all the teachers at my school truly cared about me. They noticed me for some reason, and encouraged me to do my very best. And in spite of such a tough assortment of students, I somehow just got along with everyone, I felt I really belonged, and I also usually felt safe in that school. I guess it could be said I flourished there.

When my parents found out I was at the top of my class, their attitude finally changed. From that point onward they started putting pressure on me to excel – but I just ignored them. I didn't want any of their parental pressure, I was the hardest child for them. I was quiet, but also hard-headed and even subtly disobedient in my own ways. I definitely had my own mind. They might say do this or do that, and I would listen – but then I'd just go off and do my own thing.

Along with expecting me to come right home after school to take care of my brothers and sisters, my parents were very afraid that if I hung out on campus after school, I might end up pregnant and ruin my future. There were a lot of teenage pregnancies. My parents didn't want me to look sexy when I went to school – but that wasn't an issue, I didn't have a lot of clothes, I just had two pairs of pants and I wore the same thing over and over to school.

Besides, in high school a lot of people thought I was such an ugly skinny gangly girl, like Olive Oil in the cartoons, a gawky flamingo – no style, no boobs, no nothing. Especially in a city like Lawrence which was mostly Puerto Rican and Dominicans where the men love their women curvaceous. I was nothing like that.

During that time my parents had a fourth child who was a toddler when I was in high school. Since my parents were working a lot, they needed me to come home immediately after school. I was the responsible elder child who was supposed to always be there to help run our household. I guess that was why I developed all my over-strong habits of constant cleaning and efficiently managing young children.

But like I said, I often defied them. I joined the cross-country team and high-jumped for the track team and really loved it – I just had to have a bit of my own life. My parents were very upset, they thought I was such a bad girl for not listening to them and helping them out all the time. But I was, and still am, very hard-headed.

So yeah, Lawrence was a really fabulous place for me. I didn't know what wealth was, I just knew that everyone lived the same way as we did. We all went to the same school, we all lived the same, it was our city and we knew it was different but hey, different is good, right? You just obviously had to make sure you locked your doors, and you didn't put your nose where it shouldn't be. You had to be street smart – then you'd be okay. It felt like a utopia, even though from the outside it surely didn't. And during that period of my life, I can readily say that I was genuinely happy.

PART FOUR

~~~~~~~~~~~~~

Bowdoin Traumas
~~~~~~~~~~~~~

Chapter Five

I only started to realize that I was living submerged in a less than ideal situation when I went out of Lawrence to attend a summer program at Phillips Academy and also one at Tufts University. People would comment on how I was from such a terribly poor city, or they'd notice that I had no money to spend.

Then when I got to Bowdoin College, which was quite a rich-person college, I realized all of this acutely. I'd been valedictorian in high school which usually meant I'd get into an Ivy League school. But I was passed over by the Ivy Leagues. I did get into Brown off the waiting list, but the ultimate decision of where I would go to college came down to who would offer me the most financial assistance – and that was Bowdoin up in the sticks in Maine.

Bowdoin was also the only place where I felt welcomed when I first visited. One of the admission officers, a kind woman named Karen, was especially enthusiastic to meet me. I'd been unable to write a good essay for my application, I was as usual scared of writing, I still didn't know how to write well, I'd for some reason never studied grammar at all until I studied French grammar at Bowdoin, and finally started to comprehend what sentence construction and tenses and so forth were all about.

Being so afraid to write essays, on my application to Bowdoin I instead wrote them a poem. I don't remember the poem but it was about being free in spirit like Huckleberry Finn and 'running around committing many a venial sins'. I remember that one verse very well – I loved Huckleberry Finn and admired how he was so wild and adventurous. In high school I was often living vicariously through Huckleberry Finn. Externally I didn't have his kind of life at all, but in my imagination and heart I definitely did.

Karen loved the poem, and her warm welcome kind of sold me on Bowdoin, along with talking with Haitian student Roodly who showed me around campus, and a hilariously wonderful gay Cape Verdean prospective student named Gabe who insisted that I come to Bowdoin with him. Their friendly openness, along with the fact that the school gave me such a huge financial aid package, helped me decide on Bowdoin.

Other schools like Brown barely offered me anything. When I got off the waiting list at Brown I called them up, asking if I could receive more financial aid. The person on the phone said no, they had already maxed out for all the regular admits. She also decided to let me know that getting into Brown was an investment into my future, and well worth taking on a sizeable student loan. But such a loan was unfathomable for my parents who lived paycheck to paycheck just to cover their necessities.

I took that attitude I encountered at Brown as a snub, a negative, so I then focused most of my attention on Bowdoin. I wasn't as enthusiastic to go there for college as I guess I should have been – I wanted to attend a bigger university where there would be a lot more diversity, including some students with backgrounds a bit more like mine.

For the same reasons my parents had decided to settle down in Lawrence rather than Shrewsbury, I too wanted to be in a place where there was a higher chance of fitting in and not being related to as an outsider. Put bluntly, I didn't want to go to a mostly all-white school like Bowdoin – but in the end Bowdoin was all that my parents could afford.

While trying to make my decision, I remember talking about Bowdoin with the football coach at my high school in Lawrence. Mr. Reusch happened to be the brother of that teacher from middle school who'd introduced me to *Jane Eyre*. I was in the elevator going down from the top floor of the school building with Mr. Reusch, in the spring of my senior year, and he said to me: "Mai, go to Bowdoin. Trust me. You can go to any other place in the world later on, but at Bowdoin you'll live in Maine and get to experience that special small college life."

When August came and it was time for me to attend the freshman Bowdoin orientation week, I had somehow developed quite a negative attitude toward the place even though I'd accepted its generous offer to attend. So I opted out of going on the traditional freshman orientation trip to meet my classmates. I decided instead to fly to Seattle, stay with my aunt there for a week or two, and revisit my early childhood haunts. But after that trip I finally had to go face Bowdoin.

I admit that from the first, I approached Bowdoin with this predisposition that I didn't want to be there. I felt that I was being forced by my parents and our low socio-economic status to go off into the boonies in rural Maine to endure four long years of very isolated college life. And every little thing that happened when I got to Bowdoin reinforced my negative attitude toward the place.

On my very first day there, as I was moving in, I met this white guy who asked me where I was from, and when I told him I was from Lawrence he retorted with, "Oh, so you must have gotten in here because of affirmative action." I reflexively mumbled to myself, "You fuckin' asshole," but as usual I didn't express my feelings. I just walked away – but that casual slight hurt me and did nothing to improve my feelings of being stuck at this place.

And here's another thing that developed as if on its own when I started living on the Bowdoin campus that first autumn. I defensively started to act a bit bitchy. I assumed people were putting me down for who I was, so I started doing the same to them. All while I was growing up and even in high school, I didn't really have negative feelings about people in general. I guess I'd mostly assumed my father's Buddhist attitude of accepting everyone just as they were and not judging them.

But at Bowdoin, for the first time I started to develop negative put-down judgmental feelings toward various people. I didn't like being that way, it didn't feel good – but I found myself going around swearing under my breath at people, thinking put-down hostile thoughts about their looks, their heritage, their attitudes and so forth. As I advanced through my first lonely months at Bowdoin I often caught myself actively consumed in this new habit of dissing people – and I'd be shocked at myself. I had no idea I could harbor such negative and even cruel feelings.

I think I can honestly say that it wasn't until Bowdoin that I felt the ugly emotion of sneering hatred inside me, the poisonous mental pattern of indulging in bitterness, hostility and judgment. And I think it was also the first time I started hating myself, and feeling regularly down and depressed. I'd never felt that way in high school or middle school, I never thought of myself or others in such outright negative terms.

When I arrived at my assigned dorm that first day on campus I discovered that my roommates had already claimed the best beds – and my reaction to that was to say to myself, 'well, everything is already starting off on the wrong foot'. And when one of those roommates asked me where I was from and I told her and she said "Oh, well we'll probably do better than you because we went to better schools." I thought, 'okay, there's another reason why I'm not going to like it here'.

After a few more similar encounters, I just didn't want to meet anyone. I felt so totally out of place with all these puffed-up white people so casually judging me as coming from the wrong side of the tracks. I'd think back to all my high school friends and teachers, and wish I was back there, not here. In retrospect I can analyze my unexpected negative thoughts and feelings as an expression of my own self-deprecating socio-economic fears. Perhaps in fact I wasn't good enough to be hanging out with these oh-so-clever top-notch children of privilege from much higher stations in life than myself. But back then I lacked any such self-reflective powers.

To start the year off, we all had to go to the college chapel and attend a formal convocation. I remember my roommates and I sitting on a long bench or pew where there was lots of room for others to join us. And at that moment an encounter happened that would reverberate, well, through the rest of my whole life. I watched a handsome tall white guy with long brown hair walk by and look right at me – and then decide to go sit somewhere else rather than beside me.

He was not the typical Bowdoin preppy white kid. He had an exotic foreign look that could pass him off as Persian, Eastern European, Pakistani or Mediterranean. He wasn't wearing the latest J.Crew or L.L.Bean attire, but rather a frumpy T-shirt and jeans too roomy for his slender build. I vaguely remembered having already exchanged names with him but I couldn't recall anything except that the name was quite unusual, something like Archimedes or Arcadia.

In any case I thought to myself, "Oh, okay. I guess I somehow just wasn't good enough for him to sit next to me." Like I said, I'd never had those defensive biting kinds of thoughts before coming to Bowdoin, and I didn't know why they were coming to me out of the blue now – the whole situation felt deeply confusing and upsetting. And I especially felt confused about that tall gangly man who'd decided not to sit beside me at convocation.

And so my college life began. Feeling like an outcast, I found myself not even wanting to go to the dining hall. All I did was go to classes and come back to my dorm room. I'd been fairly popular in high school, I'd made friends easily. But in this new environment with such very different students, I did the opposite. I avoided conversations, I refused offers of friendship, especially with the young women around me.

And, perhaps because of my unwarranted pushing-away from a number of women in my class, and also an unexpected sexual attraction a number of the young male students had aimed my way, I became vaguely aware of gossip flying around about me – about how I was a bit of a sleep-around slutty girl doing all sorts of illicit things off somewhere in the dark when everyone else was doing their regular accepted social things.

This totally untrue sexual reputation was really hard for me to take, and it only compounded my feelings of hating being at Bowdoin. I was in a vicious cycle of feeling I didn't fit in, and therefore retreating and being accused of doing all sorts of things that in fact I wasn't. I felt more and more confused, unwanted, insecure and insufficient. I was always on the periphery, an outcast at this cold and depressing college as the weather in Maine got bleaker and more depressing and winter approached.

I know I'm saying this rather melodramatically, and no, it wasn't all so bad of course. I had my ups and downs. But I admit that my upsurging spirit took a big hit when I went to college. Perhaps I would have had a similar down period at any college away from my family. All I knew back then was that a dark pressured weight seemed to come suddenly over me and push me down, keep me contracted.

I had fragments of childhood memories rise up when I felt low – there was something from my past, or the past of my parents or even my whole country, that was reacting to my present situation. I mean, what was I doing, a representative of my old country's civilization, playing this crazy game of trying to fit in to this ritzy American East Coast society?

I can also admit that I had anger issues at Bowdoin. I felt under pressure and so I'd release that pressure with some aggressive feelings. I was often a live wire, skinny but verbally explosive. For instance I would say 'fuck you' all the time. I think it could be said that I had a chip on my shoulder. I don't know, perhaps I felt inferior like therapists have told me, and so I acted superior, you know. The truth was, my feelings were so complicated I couldn't figure them out at all – I was just struggling to hold my own.

And probably my social identity, my sense of who I was, had become so very deeply rooted back in high school where we'd all talked like that, talked tough because the hood was in fact tough. These white kids here at Bowdoin had probably never been in a scuffle, never worked things out with their fists. They were so soft, and yet they had the nerve to put me down – when street-wise I was so far beyond them, you know. At least those were the kind of thoughts that would flow through my mind.

Even now I'm a natural swearer, it's hard for me to hold my tongue. My whole lower-class ruffian fighting attitude and raw edgy spirit, my way of relating, had been ingrained deep into me way back when I'd seriously had to be tough.

I guess basically at a 'nice' college like Bowdoin, people simply didn't know how to take me. The freshman dean must have gotten word that I was having a hard time, because she finally had me go to talk with a therapist downtown – but after just one session I realized that the guy just didn't have a clue regarding what I was going through.

Really. He just sat there looking bored when I explained that I was a barely-recovering refugee from Vietnam who was now suddenly stuck in this all-white preppy school. I'm sure I was being very defensive in how I colored my story, but from his neutral reveal-nothing words of psychological advice he showed that he had no idea how to help me – and in fact I actually wasn't looking for help. I didn't believe anyone would be able to resolve this situation, these feelings, for me.

I often allowed my mind to escape all these bothersome thoughts and feelings by just gazing out from the top floor of Coles Tower during my English classes, letting myself become mesmerized by the vibrant shimmering hues of fall leaves being gently touched by a slight breeze. It was always ephemeral, that momentary feeling of relaxed contentment and sudden escape from the challenges of being at Bowdoin. Those momentary inner escapes during my English seminar somehow made the whole situation well worth the struggle.

I found several other ways to gain some control over my feelings and my body. One was to bury myself in my textbooks, absorbing any deeper insights that could be found if I read a chapter, in Chemistry for instance, several times. People thought I was crazy to do that, to work so hard. But I loved how I could transport myself anywhere I wanted through reading books. I really did love studying!

The other thing I did that might perhaps seem a bit weird was I usually made a visit to the bathroom after a meal and gagged myself to throw up what I'd eaten. I was skinny already but somehow I just did this thing, there was satisfaction in doing it – in throwing up what had been stuffed down into me.

My mom caught me doing this one day when I was back home for a holiday vacation. She quite nonchalantly confronted me by reminding me that food was hard to come by and shouldn't be wasted. My parents could feel the difficult times I was having in college, but they kept silent for the most part.

When things got bad with an argument I had with one of the men who were flirting around with me, the school reached out to my parents to let them know I was having some conflicts, especially on weekends. My mom and dad immediately came to talk with me – and then they thought they'd solved the problem by pooling some money to get me a used Jeep Grand Cherokee that I used to escape Bowdoin every weekend.

I'd regularly drive two hours and stay at home for a couple of nights, rather than hanging out on campus and – well, getting into who knows what kind of trouble. I'd head home after chemistry lab on Friday night and come back to Bowdoin on Sunday afternoon. This was my particular way to run away from a situation where I might have met new people and experienced college the way students usually did. But I think it helped me.

Even with the support of several new male friends I made on campus, and my weekend escapes home, I often found myself slipping into depression episodes that became harder and harder for me to handle. There were too many times when I'd just retreat entirely and brood alone in my dorm. During those times I'd scarcely eat anything for days on end.

I'd sometimes get so down about life in general that I didn't even go to my classes. And I'd also sometimes become so upset or worried about something or someone that I'd start gasping and hyperventilating, hardly be able to breathe at all. Later on in my life I would be diagnosed with asthma, and even back in California I'd had terrible breathing attacks – which no one knew how to treat.

During one of these depressed episodes at Bowdoin I got so down and out that I actually began having serious thoughts about suicide. I remember one time when I hadn't eaten for days and I collapsed down, out of breath and mostly unconscious. Luckily someone found me in this condition and quickly ran to get help for me.

My savior just happened to be that same dark-haired white kid who lived below me, the same guy who'd chosen not to sit next to someone like me at the college convocation. After that bothersome incident this tall guy, whose name was Arkady, started casually spending time with me here and there, coming up to my dorm room to chat about this and that, or me going down to his room.

We seemed in many ways to be a total mismatch, always at odds with each other. We'd argue about the stupidest shit, like 'is Lawrence a city or a town?' But somehow through our banging heads over many small things we started to get to know each other more and more. At deeper levels we quite unconsciously began to form a special unique friendship bond.

I initially thought that Arkady was totally snobby, privileged, condescending and so forth. I didn't know anything at first about what he'd come through in his childhood. He didn't talk hardly at all about his background. Like me he had a slight accent and I knew it was from Europe, but I didn't know where at first.

Since I usually didn't leave my room that first year except for classes, I exercised in my room, mostly speed jump roping. And my roommate was often bouncing a ball. Arkady, living right below us, would come fuming up the stairs and ask if we could stop making so much damn noise. We'd mostly ignore him and tell him that we're not doing anything as we stood there holding evidence in our hands – and often we'd continue with our activities once he was gone. You know, that freshman banter sort of relating.

While I myself didn't want to be judged, here I was judging someone – I thought he was ugly, and he thought I was ugly. He once asked me, as he stared me up and down, "Why are Asian women flat like a wall?" I think he was genuinely curious about this question. He couldn't understand why we had no boobs, no butts, and small noses.

Of course, I had to say something, and I followed up his comments about my looks with some cursing and name calling. He would retort that he liked Russian women, they were all so curvaceous, you know, triple D's and whatnot. And every time he made that type of comment I'd come back at him with "Why do you Jews have such big noses?" He always proudly responded, "Well the air is free."

Our exchanges now sound acrid and racist and all the rest, but even though we constantly butted heads, we didn't get hurt from our freshman banter. I did get annoyed at times but mostly we were just playing, we'd find something weird about each other and kind of poke fun at each other. I thought his name was too long. My first name is just one syllable and three letters. I told Arkady that I didn't have the time and breath to say his whole name, so I decided to call him Ark – and it stuck, Ark is now what lots of people, mostly close friends and family, call him today.

As I'd learn, Ark is not the type of person to talk openly about his feelings – not with anyone. But still he's such an interesting person. He's in fact quite good looking but that's not how I saw him when we were in college. Ironically one time in our freshman year, a friend asked me what my ideal guy would look like. This happened in my dorm room and I proceeded to describe my ideal guy: “Tall, dark, handsome, strong cheeks, maybe in a suit.” Right then by coincidence Arkady walked into the room wearing a suit, hair slicked back and looking exactly how I’d described my ideal man. He was heading off for an interview or something that required a suit. I quickly said, “But no – certainly not him!”

On the surface, Arkady was this annoying, sort of stuck-up kid from a wealthy town, Brookline, MA. But underneath, he was a Russian Jewish immigrant – he came to the U.S. when he was eleven. The reality was that after immigrating he’d grown up in a rent-control apartment on Short Street off of Beacon Street in Brookline. His father was a taxicab driver and his mom traveled hours each day as a pharmacy technician.

Most people don’t know that just before coming to America, Arkady at eleven years had hustled on Italian beaches to sell Russian items to help his family during their temporary layover in Italy. My family had our parallel experiences in that Indonesian refugee camp of Galang. I felt a new level of respect when he privately shared this and other humbling stories such as being made fun of for wearing one pair of pants to school every day when he first came to the U.S.

Chapter Six

I did struggle a bit academically at Bowdoin. To put it mildly, I was not well prepared for the academic rigor at Bowdoin, especially when it came to writing course papers and such. I did quite well in science and math, but I also had to take liberal arts requirements that forced me to express myself in writing. I was so scared of writing an essay or report that I went several nights without sleeping hardly at all.

I just couldn't understand how someone could write ten pages in the same time it took me to write only one page – and their ten pages often sounded like a work of art torn from the pages of Nabokov. Mine, on the other hand, felt constricted and forced, in the same tight tone that I spoke – carefully thought through, reviewed, edited and re-edited. Even a hint of personality and flow were missing, not to mention any adherence to the rules of grammar.

As expected, during my freshman year I did well in science and math, getting high grades – but my courses that required writing lowered my grade point average. Then in an English seminar on black-and-white cinema, I just gave up trying to write 'correctly' and instead literally wrote whatever was on my mind about all the sexual innuendos from Marilyn Monroe's "I always get the fuzzy end of the lollipop," to "like Jell-O on springs" in *Some Like It Hot.* I didn't hold back at all with my foul language and blunt sexual analysis. I took the risk of letting my true thoughts flow onto written pages without inhibition, feeling I didn't really have anything to lose, that I'd get a bad grade anyway.

But that was my first A for a paper, and it gave me a beginning taste of something that I was barely prepared for. I was reminded of my love of novels from way back in junior high school, and after that class I became quite curious about topics and courses outside of math and science. In fact, this was when I took the plunge and began my journey into the humanities. I switched my major in that direction and probably forever changed my career trajectory.

I shifted majors from science to the humanities for two main reasons. First of all, I was determined to conquer my fear of and weakness in writing – it loomed as my primary hindrance to a successful future in America. And secondly, I really hungered to explore the world beyond numbers and equations. The humanities offered me a chance to look at human beings and study expert interpretations and judgments regarding what human beings did and why they did it. Perhaps I'd fit into that niche in college.

It's often said that going to college should be the best time of your life. After all, you're free from your parents for the first time (if you didn't go to a boarding school). You've left the nest to explore the world around you – and you're free to risk and experiment, to fail and succeed and fail and succeed again. You're probably going to meet your future best friends, you'll fall in love and out of love, you'll explore exciting new subjects, new music, new everything – college should be just great!

And I admit now that I had some of these uplifting encounters and experiences at Bowdoin. I don't mean to dwell on the negative. But there's no way around the fact that I plunged too often into heavy depression. Somehow my refugee past caught up with me when I left my Vietnamese home for an almost exactly opposite cultural environment.

I'm still not sure how much I projected my own self-deprecating attitudes onto my classmates, but in college it was made clear to me, whether spoken or unspoken, that I did not belong – that I was just too different. Over and over I picked up attitudes around me that I was not someone to be associated with as a friend. Like I said, before attending Bowdoin my status as a poor refugee had felt normal because everyone around me was in the same condition. But when I arrived at Bowdoin I was made quickly aware that my entire identity, my core sense of self, was in negative contrast to almost everyone else around me.

I studied French in college, perhaps because Vietnam had been colonized not by the British or the Germans or the Spanish or the Portuguese, but by the French. That language had become the second language of many of my people, especially those like my parents who had somewhat adapted to French rule. Also, considering my depressive tendencies, I was very strongly drawn to the existential philosophy of the French books I began delving into, such as Albert Camus' book *L'étranger* (The Stranger).

It was overly easy for me to identify with that novel's blunt anti-hero, Meursault, who was a total outsider living on the extreme periphery of his society. But unlike Meursault, I had already lost that protective sense of simplicity in life which he portrayed. Instead, I began to ponder ad infinitum about who I was, what it means to be different, and why I was perceived as and ridiculed for being different.

My entire sense of self-esteem crashed during that first year I was in college. Like I said, I began to experience almost violent feelings of hatred and repulsion for things, people, and myself. At heart I guess I simply didn't want to be there in Brunswick – and I felt hopelessly imprisoned. Was this actually the end result of the path my life had naturally followed up until now?

In middle school and high school I'd always seized every opportunity I could find to learn about something new. And during that period of my life minor negative things that happened hadn't much bothered me. But now it seemed that absolutely everything about college life grated against my nerves. What a terrible place! Such repulsive people! Wow, did I become negative!

But honestly, I didn't purposely choose to sink into such blatant negativity and hostility – it just developed all on its own inside me. When I got to Bowdoin I didn't even know what depression was, and I'd certainly never before experienced those weird debilitating feelings of abject loss and total hopelessness. The sinking sensation of crashing suddenly down into despair just snuck up and took over my soul. And … I had no idea how to fight back.

I might mention that the flood of depressing songs of that period didn't help. Just turning on the radio depressed me with all the alternative rock lyrics pulling my mood even further down. And there was also the fashion style on campus. One of the things that shocked my classmates was my way of dressing. I didn't don J.Crew and L.L.Bean. That's what rich kids wore – but I didn't have a budget to keep up with them, so perhaps I convinced myself I didn't want to look like them anyway.

The truth was that I didn't have many outfits, and most of what I wore came from thrift stores. My clothes back then very much resembled today's style – fitted pants and jeans, form-fitting shirts, trendy outfits. If I were to wear those clothes on the Bowdoin campus these days I would fit in easily. I guess I was just ahead of my time, at least for Bowdoin.

On the other hand, and perhaps because of my differences, being at Bowdoin was really very good for me. I was forced to confront, accept and finally embrace who I authentically was – what I liked and what I didn't like. I began the essential soul process of coming into my own self, finding my honest personal identity – finding love, learning hate.

In a sense, leaving my family and high-school nest and breaking free from my traditional Vietnamese upbringing allowed me, or rather forced me, to explore outside the limited refugee bubble I was so accustomed to. And looking back in retrospect, and only in retrospect, I can say that college was not only the worst but also the best experience for me – because I became … me.

Understandably, by the middle of my freshman year I wanted to transfer out – but when I spoke with my father about leaving Bowdoin he didn't approve, he wanted me to finish what I'd started. He felt that if I quit or transferred, it would come across as failure – not only for me but for him and for our community. How could his daughter, the honored high-school valedictorian, quit college?

Dad also loved Bowdoin, having visited the campus and seen how the school welcomed me with open arms and given me such a generous scholarship package. He insisted that their generosity was something to be grateful for, in light of where we came from – and that if my family had been able to endure such excruciating physical and mental suffering for so long, that my challenges with Bowdoin should be the least of my worries, just another obstacle to overcome as part of life.

I finally decided to accept his advice and just push through Bowdoin, even finish up strong academically if at all possible. I became determined to get strong and even like where I was, and to get the most out of college no matter how difficult that challenge seemed.

In retrospect, how different my life would have flowed if I'd gone elsewhere my sophomore year. Who I am today and who I have in my circle of family and friends would certainly have been significantly altered. At Bowdoin, by getting so banged around and then ending up with many enduring relationships, I managed to learn the biggest lesson of all – that friendships are everything in life.

Those friendships – with Arkady, Brian, Naeem, Gabe, Jeff, My, Roodly, and a few others – are still meaningful in my present life. You'll notice that the names are all male, I just naturally got along with them rather than the women at Bowdoin, which was mostly why I got a reputation for being a sleep-around girl on campus. But honestly it was just that I could shoot the shit with those guys without fearing judgement and without having to try to learn all the nonsense most of the women on campus seemed to believe about proper etiquette.

Through all our rough talk and emotional honesty, these guys made me feel safe, they accepted me for who I was back then and who I still am today. Also of note is that most of my friends in college were either people of color or people who were open to outsiders like me. I didn't have friends from the popular or mainstream groups. At times, I dated guys in the hip social and athletic circles on campus, but mostly I hid out in dorm rooms with my tight little gang.

I suppose hanging with only guys in college, especially optically, sent the wrong message – and this was the very thing my parents had wanted me to avoid. It definitely wasn't 'good girl' behavior to continually hang out behind closed doors with a bunch of guys, and me the only girl. I was providing a lot of gossip fodder, even if it wasn't true, for the community to talk behind my back about me. And yeah, I wore tight fitting clothes and was probably seen as overly sexy. But that was just who I was and how I wanted to express myself.

And I honestly didn't give a damn about all the gossip – I was like, fuck that. Those girls weren't my friends, I didn't need them and they never seemed to need me. Internally, of course I wanted to escape the rumors being spread, but what was I to do? Certainly not reject my guy friends and buy new boring clothes and curb my tongue and all that.

With my male friends, I formed unique bonds with each of them. Quite probably I wouldn't have made it through Bowdoin if it weren't for them. I've already told you a bit about Arkady. And it was Brian who'd asked me who my ideal guy would be. Brian was a white kid from Lewiston, Maine and despite his skin color, I swear he was my Vietnamese brother from a different mother.

My group of Bowdoin friends developed our special type of joking banter that, from the outside perhaps, seemed a bit bizarre – but we loved it. We expressed our deeper feelings through our rough male humor. Brian for instance would always shout hellos to me when we met on campus by using an insider joke-greeting which I'd patiently taught him to say in Vietnamese: "Mai ăn một khúc cứt!" And I would laughingly tell him back the same thing in Vietnamese: "Brian, you eat shit!"

I did find one close Vietnamese friend at Bowdoin, also almost a brother from a different mother. The first time I met My, who was a class ahead of me, he walked right up to me with a limp in front of Moulton Union wearing baggy clothes and a puffy jacket and said, "Wassup?!?" That standard 'hood greeting', and his put-on casual walk with the slight fake limp, was familiar to me from back in Lawrence. It was cool, a sign that you were carrying too much dough (aka cash), a piece (aka weapon), or other things in your pocket weighing one side of you down.

My and I (yes, that was his name, we were My and Mai) felt an immediate bond and a sense of shared understanding in that first brief exchange, and our friendship was instantly born right then and there. As fellow Vietnamese refugees we had so much in common to talk about. And although we didn't often have deep heart-to-heart conversations, My always had my back, he was there if I needed anything.

One time later on I think he got quite upset with me – because I made his mother cry. I was helping a Harvard grad conduct interviews with Vietnamese refugees, and My's mom graciously offered to share her escape story. Unfortunately my questioning began to bring to mind some agonizing escape memories that were soon followed by tears. I felt very bad about that, and vowed to be more careful and considerate with people who'd suffered through such traumatic times.

My was good friends with Roodly, whom I mentioned earlier had been my student guide when I came to visit campus my senior year of high school. Roodly spoke with a soothing Creole voice that seemed to calm me down even in my most upset or anxious moments. We both studied French and found much joy in that department because the professors made us feel like we belonged.

Whenever I was down and needed a reason to be at Bowdoin, Roodly always found a way to confirm that I'd made the right choice. Looking back, I'm amazed at how I was somehow almost always helped at heart levels when I really needed it. In certain ways I was a total mess in college – and so often there was someone there to offer me their attention and compassion.

Jeff was also good friends with Roodly. Jeff was this tall, lanky, bespectacled Korean kid. He always started smiling and joking when he saw me. One day, he asked me to be his friendly date to some school ball. It was one of my first social outings at Bowdoin. I wasn't into social events at the school, but I stayed on campus that weekend to attend the ball with Jeff.

He came to pick me up in a tux and I'd found myself a red satin spaghetti-strap dress from a discount store for the occasion. We actually had a blast together, awkwardly moving along to the beat of Count Basie band music performed live by some local group. That was the night I started to learn about and enjoy this type of music, which was quite different from the hip hop, rap, and slow jams that I grew up with. I quickly began developing a love for jazz music which became my go-to relief when my soul needed it.

I also met another kid, a very interesting, quirky guy named Naeem who was from Pakistan. He was super tall, skinny and somewhat dorky, and he walked around campus dressed in an all-white traditional outfit (a *kurta* pajama) with traditional pointy leather shoes like Aladdin, and a Muslim cap (*taqiyah*). He had a delightfully wicked tongue which was often hilarious and super geeky.

Naeem and I got along so well despite our different worlds. One weekend he invited a group of his former high school friends from Aitchison College, an elite all-boys high school in Pakistan, to gather at Bowdoin. Naeem invited me to join him and this somewhat large group of male friends. I was the only female and the only non-Pakistani hanging out with all these guys at a bowling alley – and we had so much fun.

There was another person, Gabe, whom I met on that visiting trip to Bowdoin my senior year in high school and helped convinced me to come join him as freshmen. Gabe had these gorgeous light hazel eyes and caramel skin from his mixed ancestry of Portuguese and indigenous natives from the Cape Verde islands off west Africa. He was vociferous in his beliefs, and he had the jolliest laugh. He was a bright gay kid who was always enthusiastically bubbly for no reason. He always lifted my spirits. Even when I disagreed with him, I was often mesmerized by how his thoughts and opinions on everything came out so eloquently and convincingly.

So yes, I had mostly male friends, and we all shared the invaluable ability to be humorous and laugh together – not at each other. I could goof around and swear and rough-house with them, mostly because of my tough background. I could be raw and make jokes about them and they wouldn't be offended. In contrast, at this level I couldn't connect with the girls at Bowdoin at all. So I greatly valued my small group of friends.

I didn't really party with any of them, we just hung out together. We'd have pizza during the week, and do a dinner when I was on campus for weekends. These guys just loved me for who I was – and that kind of acceptance was so hard to find at Bowdoin back then, and perhaps to find anyplace at any time.

Chapter Seven

In reflection, I really don't know why I went around hating Bowdoin so much – after all, I had such good friends and I also had such a great academic experience. I understand that these days, as opposed to back then 25 years ago, students who feel alienated for one reason or another can now get compassionate help from the college staff in adjusting to the new social environment. Solutions can now be found. I'm very pleased to hear this.

But at that time I guess no one could recognize that I was in trouble, or if they did, they didn't know to help me. My freshman year wasn't so bad in retrospect, but my sophomore year got really very tough because my mood swings often became extreme. For instance on a good mood day, if there was an exam I would get maybe one question wrong or none at all. I could ace those exams because I worked hard preparing, and made sure that on all fronts I was doing very well.

But when I found myself slipping into one of my down-swings I would quickly enter a mental phase where I couldn't focus on anything academic at all, I couldn't force myself to study before an exam – and so of course I'd totally fail the test. This meant that my assignments and my exam grades within a course would be seriously inconsistent, all over the place.

When I was mentally stable and feeling happy, life was mostly good. That's why I know I shouldn't complain about that year – after all, I enjoyed life greatly when I was in good spirits and riding a high. But more and more often I just couldn't study, something unseen would prevent me from focusing. I still can't tell you what it was, but I felt like I was caught right in the vortex of an interior black hole of some sort. I would just sit with a blank mind for hours, staring at my textbook – and then at some point I would start to cry for no reason at all. I was really a big mess of unpredictable seriously-depressed emotions.

My sophomore year was especially challenging because I took more courses than most other students did – five courses a semester, including the hardest courses like Organic Chemistry and difficult essay-based courses. Taking Organic Chemistry wasn't hard for me, it was the writing courses. I was determined to overcome my writing difficulties, so instead of majoring in science and math, as I mentioned earlier, I chose Government and French – but I also wanted to keep my options open in science and pre-med.

Because I was having such a rough time with inconsistent grades, the Dean for our class tried to convince me to drop one of the courses so that I could do better academically, and also enjoy school a little bit more. But I was stubborn and refused to give up a course. She decided to talk to my friends, Arkady and Brian and a few others – and I finally gave in, especially to Arkady, and dropped Organic Chemistry, even though I was one of the few students doing well in that course.

I remember many years later when I had career visions of going into healthcare, how I sometimes seriously resented Arkady's influence intensely – because he'd pushed me to drop the required

Organic Chemistry credits that I needed to move in that career direction. But to be honest, it was the best thing.

Dropping Organic Chemistry took a lot of pressure off my shoulders. It allowed me to breathe and focus on the courses that I enjoyed. I actually didn't enjoy Organic Chemistry – I mean, who actually loves putting molecules together? The only thing I remember from Organic Chemistry is how certain atoms attach to each other, one from the front and the other from the rear – and I remember that only because I used it in a dirty joke with my friends.

But even with my reduced course load I still didn't like school and I still didn't like most of the students who surrounded me every day. I still wanted to escape. So when the opportunity came to study abroad, I applied immediately for my junior year and thank goodness, I got accepted.

I was so excited to fly away from Bowdoin that I very much wanted to study the whole junior year abroad. But realistically I just didn't have the money, there was no way I could survive in another country for an entire year on my college stipend. So I opted for just one semester. I held onto that looming new experience coming in my junior year, and did my best to survive the rest of my sophomore year…

One thing that helped me during my sophomore year was joining the Asian Student Association. We did fun things like putting on spoof fashion shows. This was when I found out something new about my natural talents – I was quite good at organizing and leading a group. But even those good social times were masked by my recurrent bouts of depression. I still don't remember how I managed to get by with my grades.

My parents perhaps saw that I was struggling in college, but I don't remember any help from their side, they just didn't want to talk about it. After all, their lives had been so hard – and I was expected to just keep quiet about my relatively-unimportant college problems, and somehow make it through higher education. For my parents, then and now, problems were something you just kept inside yourself.

The one thing about college that my parents were adamant about was that I wasn't to date or have a boyfriend – no romance! They wanted me to continue studying and focus on school. Absolutely no dating before marriage. They were strict traditionalists in that regard. When my parents came to visit Bowdoin and saw couples canoodling and holding hands, they would turn to me and remind me that such behavior would be unacceptable.

Little did they know that during my sophomore year I started dating a guy named Chris, an Asian from Hawaii with above-average height and the tanned skin that accompanied island living. I initially didn't really want to date him, because my mind was on someone else, a very handsome hot-shot jock who was showing interest in me at the time. When I shared this love dilemma with my friend Arkady, he highly suggested that I should give the 'good' guy a chance.

What he meant was that the handsome jock would always get the girls and probably wouldn't treat me well – and I took Arkady's advice. Chris was a senior, two years older than I was, so realistically our romance would last only a few months if it worked out, or it would be perfect if the relationship was a disaster and I wouldn't see him beyond that year. Besides, he was from an Asian heritage and so perhaps he would understand me better than a non-Asian.

I didn't plan to fall in love with Chris, and on the surface I was trying every possible way to avoid this outcome of our fling – but fairly quickly I found that my feelings were getting seriously romantic, in a way I hadn't felt before. Perhaps the deeper truth of this situation was that I fell in love with the idea of being romantically intertwined with an Asian man.

I soon found that I was in fact yearning to be close with someone who shared my same basic Asian culture and traditional family values. As the eldest child of a refugee family I had taken on certain unspoken obligations – to support my parents and siblings in any way, shape or form. I thought that I could never be in a lasting relationship with a man where that ingrained sense of family obligation would be questioned.

But with Chris also came his inherited oriental expectations of what a woman should be like in a relationship. I was expected to be very submissive and reticent – which in essence meant that I couldn't be myself. As my involvement with Chris developed, I found myself retreating into a traditional female role.

When I was with Chris I began to play an assumed role that seriously inhibited the true me. I tried to be that stereotypical Asian woman who in America helped to feed that standard racial fetish. I felt like I must never ever appear to be better than Chris in any way, and I certainly couldn't appear to be smarter. He didn't consciously place this pressure on me, it was just a role that I automatically adopted, based on my perception of how the relationship should look.

But in reality, we weren't at all compatible. I was unable to be true to myself – especially the loud, stubborn, free-spirited and domineering control-freak that seemed to be an integral part of my genetic personality. And I just couldn't relate to his family background. He was a trust-fund kid from a well-to-do family in Hawaii – and so his family and situation were the total opposite of mine. But somehow, despite the differences, I was in love with him, or at least with the idea of him as an upstanding Asian man.

Back then I completely failed to understand that race alone didn't automatically translate into a common understanding of life and partnership. Only later would I learn that, ultimately, shared experiences in a friendship would almost always transcend race, religion, sexuality and gender.

And meanwhile I always had Arkady by my side. Brian had developed other friends, so I hung out mostly with Arkady, Naeem, and Gabe. And also, there was Anand now in our circle. He was so funny and yet also so intelligent, serious and focused, and he just loved science. He was an Indian kid from Canada – and Anand and Naeem always argued about Pakistan and India.

After college, Anand would come out as gay, and so would our friend Brian. I think I loved the openly-gay Anand and Brian more than when they were playing straight in college. They were freer and more fun after they came out. I felt like I suddenly saw their true selves, the authentic guys who were now free to love however they choose to love. Feeling trapped must be the worst feeling – a feeling I knew so well.

There were also other people at Bowdoin who were friendly toward me and, looking back, I still feel love for them all – and I did have some friends who were women. But they were so brilliant, smart, and sweet – and I just wasn't like them. Therefore I didn't spend as much time with them as I did with my close circle of boys. I can now see how everyone I related with at Bowdoin really shaped me, in so many different ways.

But I was relieved when my sophomore year was finally over. Somehow I hadn't jumped off a bridge or done anything similar to put myself out of my misery when depression hit super bad – I had made it through that year and my junior year abroad was looming ahead of me. I was making good my escape! But I still had to be on campus at Bowdoin for the first semester and Arkady, who was still my best friend, would be gone for an entire year studying in London.

He came to visit before heading off, continually talking about his new girlfriend Lena who was Russian. He would excitedly tell me how she had a perfect figure, she was a triple-D. There was no doubt that Arkady loved his women to be curvaceous, and he assaulted me with all the minute details of his love life. But we also shared deep moments of tenderness together. We were as close as could be without having a sexual edge.

I was admittedly sad when Arkady left for London. We made tentative plans to see each other when I'd be in Paris after Christmas – but that seemed a long time away. Before he left for his finance-training program in Great Britain he said sincerely to me one night that whenever I needed something, he was ready to help me even if he was across the pond.

So – Arkady took off and I felt so all alone on campus. Naeem and several other good friends, thank goodness, were still there. But then I felt that heaviness and darkness which had plagued my first two years returning. I love autumn, and my courses were quite intriguing – but several times that semester I felt like something or someone had suddenly thrown a thick dank wet tarp of blackness over my head. And having captured my soul, this invisible and yet quite palpable entity of darkness was determined to drag me down into that black hole once again.

And then – thankfully it would finally ease up and I'd be free once more. When I felt the depression stalking me late at night, I'd plunge into studying for all I was worth, losing myself in self-imposed academic pressures. I'd decided to do a double major in Government and French plus a minor in Econ. I was trying to get as many courses as possible completed before spending my second semester in Paris. So I buried my head in my books, pushing myself to my limits. I got sick several times, perhaps because of the academic strain.

I didn't have many people to hang out with that semester, but there was Naeem – and we became very, very close. We were basically inseparable, hanging out and studying side-by-side when not in class. We became so close that our relationship transitioned innocently to another level. We were both basically single – he wasn't together with his girlfriend, she'd gone away for the semester and they'd decided to separate during that period.

But out of respect for her, I thought it would be a good idea to let her know that Naeem and I had had a moment together. I wanted to be transparent and honest, that was my code. Naeem took my advice and on the phone he told her that he was feeling close to me – and that honest communication would prove to be the doom of my senior year, and perhaps my friendship with Naeem.

PART FIVE

~~~~~~~~~~~~~~~

Paris / Princeton / Asia
~~~~~~~~~~~~~~~

Chapter Eight

Taking off for Paris for the second semester of my junior year was a much-needed break from Bowdoin. I had earlier in my life heavily romanticized the City of Lights thanks to movies like *Charade* where Cary Grant and Audrey Hepburn fell in love on the bateau-mouche with lights glimmering along the architecturally detailed façade of the Seine.

Before my trip and in flight toward my new temporary home, I dreamt of eating flaky croissants in cafés, falling in lust with a nice French boy, taking walks along the Seine, speaking French without an American accent. I wanted for the first time in my college experience to have that feeling of *joie de vie*, and I thought Paris would be the perfect place to find it.

I'd been so excited about Paris that I'd sent in my form for a host family super early. When I arrived in Paris I discovered that the study-abroad program had assigned me to a single woman in a one-bedroom apartment. She gave me her bed and she slept on the couch in the living room. I'd been expecting to stay with a family with children, so I was surprised and a bit disappointed – but I thought, sure, I guess I'll just roll with it.

But before I met my host, I had an incident at the airport. I'd booked the cheapest flight that arrived at the oddest time, many hours earlier than my group-pickup time. I got to Charles de Gaulle airport and stood around waiting for the whole group to arrive. As I was waiting there, I was obliviously standing next to two unattended suitcases for several hours – until a team of gendarmes came rushing up to me. They ordered me to leave the premise as they cleared the area to blow up those suitcases. That was my introduction to Paris. A bit shocked, it dawned on me that I wasn't quite ready for the reality outside of Bowdoin.

I had no particular feelings or fear from standing next to unattended suitcases. However, I felt a tinge of definite let-down upon learning that I would live with a single lady in a one-bedroom flat. My expectation versus the reality of my living situation in Paris created a sudden gap of disappointment. Having survived a tough situation at Bowdoin, I was wanting Paris to be different on so many levels.

And so it came to pass that I didn't get any experience at all of a French family. Instead I got a single lady who'd just broken up with her boyfriend. She was in her 50s and her ex-boyfriend left her for a younger woman. It seemed like that was the usual case in France, I kept hearing stories about French men leaving their wives and girlfriends for younger women.

I'd been hoping to experience a special sense of belonging in Paris through living with a host family with children whom I could hang out with – but all I got was a lonely woman. I had to attempt to speak French with her since she barely spoke English. That was a good thing because it forced me to learn to speak the language out loud – the very reason for going to France in the first place.

I was good at reading and writing French but I was afraid to speak the language, similar to my fears of speaking English. Grammar-wise I was actually better at French than English since I'd studied French grammar but never had proper training in English grammar. Even to this day, I still make mistakes in English with tenses and so forth.

My host lived in a very modest apartment not too far from the Eiffel Tower, a few blocks from Boulevard de Grenelle in the 7th arrondissement, quite near the Dupleix metro station. The neighborhood was lively, filled with the smell of fresh bread, flowers, street food and raw meat in its open-air market, *Marché de Grenelle*. These markets reminded me of the open markets in Vietnam elevated to the Parisian level.

I was hoping to experience all the usual French things like baguettes for breakfast and traditional French meals for dinner. But my host would mostly just serve me canned food. I loved canned food like Spam but was wanting a bit more while in Paris – so after a few weeks of orientation, following a boring dinner with my host I often headed out to meet up with some new friends for another meal – or I'd grab some Vietnamese spring rolls at the corner market to supplement my canned or very simply prepared home meals.

In general, in contrast to my romantic expectations, I didn't like Paris at all for the first two months I was there. I felt so lonely and I hated it! The worst part was that I couldn't connect at all with French people. I could barely speak the language and the French looked very much down on that. Because I'd studied French at Bowdoin it had been assumed that I could understand the spoken language. My course lectures were all conducted in French, and the lectures sounded like a euphony of smooth guttural words that was frankly Greek to me. I didn't know at all what the professors were saying. But then somehow, after a few weeks or perhaps a month, these harmonious foreign sounds began to be somewhat comprehensible.

That feeling of finally understanding what the other person was saying, of actually grasping a foreign language, felt like some unexpected form of enlightenment. And then my next challenge was to be understood by the French. I think we all strive to be understood by those around us, in order to feel safe and accepted at various levels of engagement. “To understand and to be understood makes our happiness on Earth,” according to a German proverb.

While in Paris I took the opportunity to explore classes that I would never take or which weren’t offered back home. One course in particular was Art History. I had no particular interest in this topic, but I thought I should try to explore a subject matter outside my usual interests and comfort zone. All of my Art History classes were conducted in museums – the Louvre, the Musée d’Orsay, Rodin and so forth – so that we could gaze in person and study every painting and statue.

Even though I got my worst college grade in Art History, it was a remarkable eye-opening experience into a world that’s usually reserved for a certain small segment of society. I literally fell in love with art as a deep expression of feelings and thoughts transformed into a story for the whole world to visualize and enjoy. This appreciation for things like art had always in my life been seen as a privileged luxury far out of reach and foreign to me. Feeling passionate about such supposedly-trivial things had not been encouraged or even allowed in my refugee background.

But now I found I’d reached a point in my life where I had achieved the privilege to study and fall in love with art. Ahh! The bad grade didn't matter, what mattered was that I suddenly had the freedom to fall in love with beauty, with creativity, with masterful artistic lines, colors, strokes, and curves.

Unlike Bowdoin, living in Paris forced me to venture outside my usual comfort zone in so many ways, ranging from unusual course selections to meeting new types of people – and particularly new types of women. My study-abroad program was actually comprised mostly of women, and two of these women, Kwanza and Lauren, helped open my eyes and heart to the French world beyond my studies. I began to be aware of my closed-minded reactions to newness in general, mostly driven by my ingrained fear of not being accepted, of being judged and discounted as a worthless refugee.

I discovered step by step that by momentarily letting go of that fear, I was able to spontaneously connect with various people in the Paris study-abroad program who were from every corner of the world. We'd meet for drinks or meals, or simply take a stroll together on the cobblestone streets through quaint neighborhoods here and there in Paris (but I learned the hard way to *fais attention* to the dog shit, as Parisians don't pick up after their dogs).

Kwanza and Lauren unknowingly helped me let my guard down and explore both myself and the world around me. They accepted me irrespective of how different I was. To be able to share my Paris experiences with them made Paris come alive for me – otherwise I might have been even more miserable than if I'd stayed at Bowdoin.

I was also lucky enough in Paris to become friends with a fellow Bowdoin classmate named Ben. Somehow being outside my college comfort zones allowed me to strike up a conversation with him one day. If it weren't for Paris I would've never hung out with someone like Ben, who was a rather handsome and charming, sometimes hilarious and very preppy white boy from a privileged background who hung out with the most popular kids at Bowdoin.

Ben and I took Art History together and spent a lot of time meeting up at various museums for classes. We soon developed an unlikely friendship and latent attraction to each other – and actually it wasn't so latent. With his infectious smile he somehow lit everyone up around him. He was open to anyone and anything, never shying away or judging a situation or a person. I guess my blindness at Bowdoin had never allowed me to see that there were people like Ben who were cool and down with people like me. He made me smile – and when I was feeling lonely we'd get together, meet up with friends and go for a drink or to a museum or just hang out. Ben showed me how to ease up and enjoy Paris!

But still, for most of the time I was alone. I had scheduled all my classes on Mondays and Tuesdays, so that basically I had five-day weekends. Since others were in classes throughout the week, I began exploring a lot of Paris neighborhoods on my own, even going into the rough neighborhoods. I'd just find a bench in a park and quietly read a book or observe the locals walking by me.

In the process of picking up the French language, I was also gaining a love and appreciation of the French philosophers – this was good timing, because I was just then trying to understand who I was, and who I might aspire to become. Day after day on those solitary benches I was free to contemplate all sorts of reasons and explanations for my existence – why I'm so bound by my cultural expectations, why I see the world the way I do, why I might be able to become more than I thought I was.

During moments of delicious aloneness I was touched by Rousseau's thoughts on solitude, Sartre's belief that we can live to be free and take responsibility for the choices we make, and Camus' deep focus on the true meaning and preciousness of life. Somehow during those quiet moments of total solitude in a foreign land, I unexpectedly began to experience faint realizations regarding who I really was, and who I wanted to be. I began to feel a new sense of self-confidence and acceptance – and I started to care less about what other people thought or said about me. I would walked away from my bench reveries with an expanded sense of identity and purpose in life.

I also began to have the urge to speak more openly with people without being so afraid to voice my own opinions. I broke down and admitted to myself that I very much wanted to open up – I didn't want any longer to be the reticent girl that I'd been raised to be, silently submissive and never outspoken. I just wanted to be me. I wanted to pursue the things I liked and wanted to do. And most of all, as I sat there alone and all on my own, I found myself remembering times in my past when I'd actually felt very good inside my own skin. I guess I yearned to return back to when I'd been in high school in Lawrence when none of those Bowdoin status things mattered.

In this regard I felt like I was living in Jean Jacques Rousseau's book *Les Rêveries du Promeneur Solitaire.* I'd recently read and loved so many French authors, particularly the philosophers – and I often thought of myself in those existentialist philosophical terms. Sitting alone on one of the many benches of Paris, watching complete strangers walking by, something inside me softened and allowed me to fall in love … with me.

For the first time I actually began to feel love in my heart for myself. I began to feel at some deep gut level a new sense of confidence in who I really was – and especially in who I could become. I also began to raise my mental curtains so that I could more fully see the world bustling all around me, and allow new people to come into my world.

Those new expansive feelings that I felt back then are why Paris still holds so much special meaning in my heart. Later on in my life, whenever serious shit might hit the fan, I would try to manage a short trip to Paris. This happened for instance several times when I'd stop over and decompress following an intense trip to Africa or the Middle East. I'd just jet in and sit on quietly at a bench all alone in that unique city, and give myself a bit of free time to re-establish my center.

Paris for me is not the Paris most others know. It's hard to explain, but it's deep. The city didn't necessarily live up to my romantic expectations – but the city itself became my love, perhaps in much the same romantic way that Owen Wilson's character Gil Pender discovered Paris in *Midnight in Paris*.

Also as I mentioned, for the very first time in my college experience I began to make some good friends with women. Often when I wasn't in retreat I'd go out and explore Paris with my new girlfriends, going to museums, grabbing Moroccan tea at a mosque, eating cheese and baguette with a glass of wine in a park. I don't know why this new ability to make female friends came into my life but I was delighted – especially because my women friends helped me grow so much internally.

Paris was for sure a city of love – everywhere I looked, couples were passionately kissing out in the open along the streets. It was so foreign to me to see this public display of physical affection. I remember standing in line one afternoon to exchange dollars for francs, and the couple ahead of me began to make out for several minutes. I wasn't sure what I should do – look down, close my eyes, celebrate their love, or what?

I certainly couldn't just stare at them even though they were right in front of me. So in that awkward moment I looked away with a smile, accepting and even embracing this carefree expression of romantic love that had been severely suppressed by my traditional Vietnamese upbringing and also the conservative American attitudes toward displaying one's affection. I found myself wondering what it would be like to be so free in expressing my feelings.

Unlike guys back at Bowdoin, French men would boldly come up to me and say, "Vous êtes très belle," and proceed to ask if I wanted to *rendez-vous* somewhere. One evening as I was standing in the train station heading home to my stop at Dupleix, a tall blond Frenchman hopped out and asked for a date. He gave me his number and hopped right back on the train. Normally back in the States this would never happen, and if it did I would've thrown the number away. It was a stranger-danger type of situation. But I called and scheduled a time for drinks and dessert in a public place, with fluttering feelings flying in my stomach, my heart swept off into a highly-romantic moment.

But although I wanted to discover lust or love or some form of romance in France, I somehow found myself regularly thinking about the Asian man back in the States who I'd at least thought I was in love with – Chris. He was living in Seattle at the time. I'd saved up for a spring break trip to travel around Europe. Instead I flew way over to Seattle to see Chris. I was not sure what I was hoping to achieve with the trip. I think I knew that nothing would develop beyond our one year together at Bowdoin.

I was embarrassed to tell my friends in Paris that I was skipping a trip around Europe just to go visit an ex-boyfriend with no clear reason except to see him. Well, I did tell Arkady who was over in London at that time. Ark and I were still best friends, our bond seemed to be continuing even though we had no idea what our future might bring. He regularly confided in me regarding his various London romances and so I phoned him and told him I was headed for Seattle.

So I flew out west and spent time with Chris – but oddly I felt quite underwhelmed by the entire experience. I don't usually regret my decisions but that was one I wished I hadn't made. I returned to Paris feeling bummed that I could have had a wanderlust adventure with my girlfriends through Europe instead of trying to reawaken romantic feelings from the past.

Upon returning to Paris I was clearly upset with myself. But I didn't want to sit around moping in my room, so my first night back in France I called up Ben to meet for dinner. Then I quickly showered and changed into my effortless Parisian miniskirt outfit, and met Ben at a restaurant on the Seine for al fresco dining.

The early evening was beautiful with the crispness of a warm springtime breeze soothing my skin as the last rays of sunlight continued to add warmth and glow to a perfect evening for dining outside. It seemed as though all of Paris was out enjoying the magic moments of that evening. I can't remember much of our discussion but I can still remember the feeling of total contentment, chatting over a great meal and good wine as we shared deep thoughts and also laughter together. Memories of my trip to Seattle disappeared as though that episode had never happened.

After dinner, we meandered along the Seine with the full moon illuminating the river and our faces. As we strolled along and continued to chat, Ben suavely said, "It would be a shame to waste a perfect romantic moment." And he was right! I let go of everything that had suppressed my latent attraction for Ben and softly yet passionately kissed him for some unknown amount of Parisian time on the cobblestone banks of the Seine.

But my Cary Grant moment with Ben on the Seine was short-lived. We went our separate ways that evening. Ben was a ladies' man, and I didn't want to be just another number. I enjoyed that memorable romantic moment for what it was, as if it'd been captured in my mind's eye by Robert Doisneau, a famous French photographer known for his pictures of couples kissing. I also didn't want to step further beyond that line of friendship with Ben, even though it was slightly too late for that. We continued to meet up as if nothing had happened – but the mutual attraction was so strong that it continued subtly even after we both returned back to Bowdoin.

All along while in Paris, as I mentioned, Arkady and I talked regularly on the phone. His birthday was coming up, he was turning twenty-one and I wanted to do something special for him – so I bought him a train ticket to the south of France for his birthday. He came over to Paris from London and we spent a bit of time wandering together around the city. We still felt very close to one another in our unique way, we very much enjoyed being together, but we also returned to our usual sibling-like bickering about the stupidest things.

After a few days of showing him around Paris, we took the train south to Nice. The weather was beautiful, it was around the end of May and everything was blooming like crazy. I knew that Arkady was still together with his Russian girlfriend from Boston – but oddly, he didn't talk about her hardly at all. We spent most of our time joking around, but also sometimes we would dive deep into talking about things like what life might be like after college.

Settling into a hotel in Nice, we sat on the rocky beach staring out over the azure blue sea, and as we relaxed, feeling totally away from everything in our past, Arkady softly and quietly began sharing some of his deeper feelings – about how hard his life had felt as a first-generation immigrant in America, struggling with no family money, zero legacy and minimal network to find a good job after graduating the following year. He mentioned several classmates whose fathers were well established in their respective fields. Being the son of a refugee taxicab driver and pharmacy-technician mother wasn't going to help him get even an interview with an investment bank, which was where he hoped to establish his career.

I sat there and listened, wishing I could help – but I was no different than him as the daughter of a mail-delivery mother and an odd-job technician father. I shared with Arkady how I had decided to go straight from Bowdoin to graduate school. I told him that I'd taken the GRE exams in Paris with this plan in mind. The future seemed difficult, but we were both determined to plow ahead and do our best to somehow transcend our shared immigrant heritage.

But despite our similar background experiences, Arkady and I couldn't have been more different. For instance I was always pinching my pennies and wanted to eat very cheaply on our short vacation in Nice, mostly grabbing street food – but Arkady wanted fancy meals in sit-down restaurants, so we got into a huge argument one evening about food.

In France they have these little Asian corner-stores where they sell prepared fried rice or spring rolls and such, and I wanted to spend just a couple of dollars and get something like that to eat. But Arkady wanted a formal sit-down meal – so finally I caved, considering that it was his birthday. We went to a restaurant but I kept grumping about the cost. Looking back, I can't believe how much I complained to him.

But we still enjoyed ourselves for the remaining days of the trip. We sparred a lot as friends but most of the time, they were just little spats and we quickly moved on. Arkady loved the beach scene but I couldn't swim and was afraid of water and hated the gritty sand of the beach. But yeah, he won, we went to the beach. It was the perfect birthday gift for Arkady after a winter in London – soaking up the sun, enjoyably surrounded by topless women. He even went swimming with one of them. I was probably the only non-topless woman on the beach. I mean, what would my mother have said if I'd bared all in public?

Chapter Nine

~~~~~~~~~~~~~~~~~~~~~~~~~~~~~~

With my emotions in a jumble regarding my confused feelings for Ark, we went back to Paris and he returned to London. A couple months later he headed back to Boston and I followed a few weeks later. Right around that time Ark's girlfriend broke up with him and he was heart-broken – and then all of a sudden he was wanting to spend all of his free time that summer with me before we headed back for our senior year at Bowdoin. But that summer dream was a no-go because I was heading south to New Jersey for a summer program at the Princeton School of Public and International Affairs (SPIA).

Back in the fall of 1998 before I'd left for Paris, the Dean of Admissions at Princeton, a wonderful man named John, had come up to Bowdoin to talk about the Princeton SPIA and its Public Policy International Affairs (PPIA) program. This was a prestigious fellowship that funded a summer at Princeton and two years of a graduate program for highly-qualified students of color wanting to explore a career in government policy.

I attended the talk and considered applying. But when I spoke with my professor about this, he informed me that being accepted would be difficult, as they demanded perfection on many fronts, hinting that I myself wasn't at that level. However, when I spoke with Arkady about the summer fellowship he encouraged me to apply. My dad did too – they both thought that I should give it a
~~~~~~~~~~~~~~~~~~~~~~~~~~~~~~

shot regardless of the outcome. There was nothing to lose in trying.

Throughout college and beyond, Arkady and my dad were always supporting my sometimes-lofty ambitions, even when others didn't. So I'd applied for the summer fellowship at Princeton right before heading off to Paris. I found out that I'd gotten in when I logged into my email one day while studying at The American Library in Paris in the spring of 1999. When I wrapped up my time in Paris that June of 1999 and returned to Lawrence, I had very little time free before heading down to Princeton for the summer.

I fell quickly in love with Princeton that summer – but it was very intense academically. The situation felt unreal from the beginning for me, to be with a group of such high-caliber students who most accepted and embraced me. I made some very close friends in the program, some of whom I still keep in contact with. Many of them actually had the same basic background as I did, identifying as Black, Indigenous, and People of Color (BIPOC). We had struggled in a variety of ways during our childhood, and this shared struggle helped us establish a mutual bond and treasured sense of closeness.

During that summer program I also became close with John and his administrative team. John had the knack of seeing the potential in young people. If it weren't for John, I don't think my dots would connect at all the way they have in my life. For instance, John soon learned of my writing and communication struggles – and he took it upon himself (with his wife Emily) to help me overcome this deficiency. I would go over to John and Emily's house to work on writing quite often during my summer at Princeton. They graciously took their time out of their busy schedules to help me. John didn't have to extend his hand and heart to me like he did, but he has continuously held to his undying commitment to help people like me in the BIPOC community who are struggling to achieve equality of opportunity in academic and government leadership roles.

Oh, how I loved being on that quiet countryside campus. I simply fell in love with Princeton, with all its lush landscaping and subtle Ivy League atmosphere – and I loved the friends I made that summer. I seemed to be fully in my element, on a non-stop high. It was the best summer of my life – but then all too soon it was over and, very sadly, I left Princeton and returned to Bowdoin to face my senior year there.

Friendship-wise it was a dreaded autumn. That one phone call I'd insisted Naeem make to his old girlfriend before I left for Paris, about that one kiss, blew up in my face. Why was I always so up-front and honest about things? That same girlfriend was back in Naeem's love life on campus again – and she told all our mutual friends how I'd betrayed her with that kiss. She vowed never to be in the same room with me ever again, and I was therefore unable to hang out with Naeem or attend gatherings if she planned to be present.

That was a monstrous vow because Naeem and Arkady were roommates that senior year, and they were my closest friends. This meant that when she was with Naeem, I wasn't allowed to be present – which meant most of the time. The result was that mutual friends were torn between her and me, and nasty rumors of me as a secret seducer took hold in too many people's minds.

In a small school like Bowdoin with mostly mutual friends, that meant I felt as shut out and isolated as I had my freshman year. This situation just sort of happened to me – and rather than fight for my reputation, I retreated silently into my studies and hung out only with Arkady and Gabe. My deep wonderful time in Paris and then at Princeton had come crashing down.

I think Naeem was as heartbroken by all of this as I was, but he was very much caught up in his romance. And to make matters worse, around October Arkady started to act very weird toward me. I couldn't understand why, so one day I just threw it out at him and asked, "Hey, what's up with you recently? Why are you being so incredibly annoying with me? Do you, uhm, like me or something?"

He was quiet. He didn't say anything. Then he finally managed to say, "Well, maybe." He fell silent again, so I pushed on. "Just what the fuck does 'maybe' mean? You either like someone or you don't." And he was like, "So okay, yeah, I do. We should try it out, being really together. It could be fun, just for a year before we graduate. I think we'd have great sex."

I said right back at him: "What are you thinking? What are you talking about? No, absolutely not. You're my brother, not my bed mate. You know how having sex can ruin a friendship."

I'm not sure if I fully believed my reaction, or if I was just being defensive and not wanting to become vulnerable at that sex level and get hurt. Anyway I just put aside his comments and we went our way. But he continued acting weird and then yeah – at some point around mid-October we hooked up one night. But it was beyond awkward for me, I felt the whole thing was really terribly wrong. I didn't want to break his heart, he seemed so genuine with his passion for me.

But I couldn't hide my own feelings, so I told him the next day that I couldn't do that again with him … and I saw the look on his face. It broke my heart to see him so wounded, so sad. I'd never seen him feeling like that before. So I gave in. "Okay, fine," I said, "we can try to give it another chance."

I think we came together and then broke up ten times that semester. But … every time I tried being that totally intimate with him, I felt like something was being violated. I wanted to tell him that being sexually intimate wasn't working out – that every time we kissed I thought of my brother, and besides, we just didn't kiss well. But I couldn't stand to see him heartbroken, so I gave it another try. I knew he wouldn't understand but for three years I'd seen him too much as a brother, as kin. It was just too weird, getting naked and so intimate. It felt to me like we were simply too close to each other to have sex. When our friend Brian found out he was grossed out for the same reason – the whole thing felt incestuous.

During that time I started applying to grad schools. I did quite well on my GRE but I still had to write my application essays, which terrified me. As usual when planning my future, I aimed for the sky with applications to great grad schools – but at the same time I felt like I was some kind of clever impostor and feared that I'd get found out and not get in anywhere.

Meanwhile I didn't have any real social outlets anymore on campus, because of the situation I described earlier. I barely saw Naeem at all, and Brian had some new friends. I mostly hung out with Arkady and Gabe. Things just weren't at all the same as before – except that Ark and I continued to study side by side in the library and in my room.

I often felt like I didn't really belong anywhere. Luckily Gabe knew how to make me lighten up and laugh. When he discovered that Arkady and I were together he told me how lucky I was to be so close with Ark. As it turned out, Gabe himself had a crush on Ark. When I realized this I told Gabe that he was welcome to have Ark anytime. We would laugh, though Ark didn't find this at all amusing.

One night when the three of us were hanging out together in Ark's apartment, I stayed up and worked, while Ark and Gabe crashed in separate beds in the other room. All of a sudden I heard Ark screaming. I ran into the bedroom and found Gabe in Ark's bed. I smiled, separated them and walked out nonchalantly. The truth was, we all loved each other, we accepted all our various quirks at levels that ran very deep – and so that kind of incident only made us laugh.

Winter break came and I went off to Vietnam on a fellowship from Bowdoin to research multinational corporations. I was so excited to return to Vietnam! And this time my grandfather purchased cases of bottled French drinking water ahead of my arrival. He was determined to prevent me from getting sick again.

It was so good for me to be back in Vietnam. I found myself feeling deeply connected to the country and especially to my relatives and their general flow of everyday life. I could relax like I never did in the States. Somehow I effortlessly left behind all the confused feelings of my Bowdoin situation. My true spirit seemed to come alive. Ark called once or twice when I was in Vietnam, but back then it was too expensive to make international calls.

Then the short Vietnam experience ended and I came flying reluctantly back to Boston. Arkady and his dad picked me up at Logan Airport. His dad only knew me as Ark's friend who needed a ride home to Lawrence. While in Vietnam I'd thought a lot about breaking up with Arkady – and I did so as soon as we were alone together. I didn't know at all how to do this, and so I think I came across as a real heartless bitch. I simply couldn't explain my true feelings, or lack of them, not even to myself – so I ended up using the excuse that I was still in love with Chris.

It's so strange how honest love can make you slip into being a deceitful liar. What I told Ark wasn't really the case at all. I simply didn't feel anything strongly romantic toward Ark, he definitely wasn't my ideal Cary Grant romantic figure that I thought I was looking for. He didn't sweep me off my feet and was anything but romantic with me. I knew he was capable of being romantic with girls, I'd seen him playing the charming entrancer with other lovers – but with me we were now more like friends with benefits. Yes, it hurt him to be rejected … but he stayed my friend.

Sometime that second semester during the cold winter days I became progressively ill, but not with any obvious disease. I thought maybe it was a lingering effect of my Vietnam trip. My whole body became stiff to where I was mostly unable to even move my fingers. I didn't know what was happening but I was hard-headed as usual and absolutely refused to go to the college infirmary. But still I remained so very strangely sick – and it was Arkady who took over and lovingly cared for me.

I couldn't stand being in a dorm room so I had rented a bedroom off campus in a beautiful century-old home of an elderly woman my senior year. My room was small, but Ark wanted to make sure that I was okay – so he slept in my room on the hardwood floor every night. Every morning he'd go to class and to the library to study, then come back to tenderly care for me, then sleep on the floor next to my bed.

And early one morning there came a moment when I turned to look at him curled up uncomfortably there on the floor … and for the very first time I truly felt I was in love. I'd never had those feelings before. While I thought I fell in love with Chris, this level of love for Ark was different. And so yes, I somehow began to fall in love with Arkady right in the midst of my sickness, seeing how much he was sacrificing and how much he cared despite my sexual vacillations. He could have been off partying or hanging out with his other friends. Instead he took care of me while my strange sickness went on for over two weeks.

Then I got so sick that Ark and Gabe had to literally carry me down from my room on the second floor and over to the hospital. I don't know what happened then. All I remember is getting treated and then feeling better and recovering. The medical diagnosis was that I'd caught an unusual viral infection of some sort.

My food situation during my senior year wasn't good. I was basically out of money for the year after spending it all in Paris, so I wasn't paying for the college meal plan. And besides, I was still having bouts of half-starving myself for no reason at all. My appetite which had been really quite good in Paris and also over in Vietnam, just seemed to disappear when I was back on campus at Bowdoin. I suppose the underlying cause of my eating disorder could have been traced back to my starved first few years of life as a refugee and my inability to control my senior-year experience, who knows.

The result was that I didn't eat regularly and seldom had any food around. I couldn't afford to be on the campus meal plan but Arkady was, and for lunch he was usually able to get two bags of food – two sandwiches, two chips and all that. He would bring me that extra bag nearly every day my senior year, even when I was pushing back from him romantically.

As I got better physically after my illness, deep down I started to feel differently toward Arkady, but I didn't really know what these new feelings were, and I couldn't express them to Ark. We just continued as friends, and off and on as lovers. My social sense of isolation at Bowdoin continued, but there was a bright light – I had a chance to act again.

In my senior year I was taking a French literature class and we were reading one of Jean Paul Sartre's plays called *Huis Clos*. Ben was in this course with me, and we acted out some scenes in the book for the class. We had to get together and practice, and that was so much fun! Ben played the guy and I was a woman walking around in some fancy gown. As we were acting, Ben would get all the way into his part and ad-lib, murmuring some sex-laden words in my ear – which only made me blush. That experience of acting again felt so liberating. I wasn't that good an actor, I'd never had any training. I just enjoyed it to the max. I got to play out qualities and feelings that otherwise I always hid.

I found myself definitely hiding some of my feelings away from Arkady. He was now being such a caring friend and lover, always willing to do anything for me but at the time I just took all that for granted – I didn't appreciate him even though he was so calm and patient with me. He often got bothered by my quirky moods but he never really got angry. Whenever I pushed back and broke up with him he would never say anything. Instead he'd do his honest best to try to understand. I admit that in my confusion, I was usually the bitch. He was just so sweet.

I truly didn't understand my own self at that point, certainly not romantically. Whenever I had those funny real love feelings for him, I tried to have the guts to share them with him – but then I'd remember that he only wanted us to date until we graduated. When I started having those deep 'in love' feelings for him after I recovered from my illness, I also knew that I didn't want our involvement to just end after Bowdoin. As usual he didn't express his feelings, so I didn't know what he was thinking about our future. We somehow just never managed to talk about that kind of thing.

I don't know about the experience of other people but for me, my college years were a non-stop whirlwind of uncertainty, unexpected mood swings and seriously-confusing intentions. For instance when Naeem came back from Pakistan after our senior-year winter break, it seemed that he had done some serious thinking about our messed-up social situation at Bowdoin – because he sent an email to a group of us.

The email talked vaguely about some friend of his, someone he didn't want to lose, someone he loved dearly but who was currently missing from his life – and he hated the situation. He didn't mention any names but it was clear to everyone that he was talking about me. And as it turned out, he had made up his mind that he was going to rebuild our friendship.

I couldn't hold back my tears upon reading this. I'd felt so terrible, being excluded from his presence. Naeem was truly like my brother from a different mother. He had been my rock at Bowdoin until our senior year, and the feeling of losing him from my life had torn me apart more than any romantic breakup with a guy. I didn't care what else happened in our senior year – from that point forward Naeem's decision to re-establish our friendship was all that mattered to me.

That email letter led us into a relationship which is even stronger now, twenty years after that reunion in college. We've been a part of each other's lives during our lowest moments, like when he was kicked out of the country after September 11th because his name was wrongly on the terrorist list. But more on that later.

And parallel with my renewed closeness with Naeem, I somehow started to fall more in love with Arkady. I still didn't know whether he was also falling truly in love with me, or just enjoying the sex and whatnot. We were from such utterly different backgrounds culturally – but we shared so much of the universal migrant experience, and that whole immigrant perspective on what life was all about.

This dimension of our relationship was somehow still very important to me. I had initially only wanted to be with an Asian man, believing that only someone from that background would be able to identify and understand my values and family obligations. After all, as the eldest daughter of a Vietnamese family, I did feel my duty to my parents, siblings and relatives. But at the same time I was the opposite of a traditionally submissive Asian wife – I was admittedly stubborn and determined to be independent.

I admit that I wanted to enjoy some romantic moments, but for me, the practicality of family obligations was ultimately important. Since puberty I'd lived vicariously through romantic comedies and so forth in order to get my dose of dreamy romance. But as mentioned before, with Arkady that romantic edge was definitely lacking. After all, we'd started out non-romantically as close friends and verbal sparring partners. I'd never been his ideal romantic partner.

Ark and I did have solid alignment around values and family. As a Russian immigrant, he strongly felt that his duty was to support and respect his parents and brother in whatever way he could. That also meant that, as a Russian Jew, he was expected to marry someone of his faith and cultural heritage.

Ark didn't even dare to tell his parents that we'd become sexually involved. Like me, he was always carrying that burden of wanting to please his parents – and as a Vietnamese I just didn't fit at all into their picture of his future, even if our values were aligned. So what was I to him anyway? I lacked the voluptuous curves and bulges he desired in a romantic partner. We were opposites on so many fronts – and we tended to argue more than discuss. What future could we possibly look forward to? No wonder my heart was confused.

Chapter Ten

~~~~~~~~~~~~~~~~~~~~~~~~~~~~

I was working one night at my computer when I received an email from Princeton saying that I had been accepted for graduate studies at SPIA, the same school I'd done my summer training with six months ago. I was suddenly screaming so loud that people wondered what was the matter. I felt instantly on top of the world – Princeton was my dream school and I was finally in! I felt accepted, literally and figuratively.

Arkady came over, asking what was going on. When I told him the news, we were jumping and shouting with joy together. And then the funny thing was that, instead of going out and celebrating, I just went right back to my studies even though they didn't really matter anymore. I wanted to finish off the year strong at least in one area of my life at Bowdoin.

Graduation in May 27, 2000 was just around the corner and I could hardly wait. I couldn't quite process my mixed feelings about Bowdoin – I'd had a fairly hard time there and I wanted to leave it all behind and move forward without holding on to any of those memories, good or bad. I was done with Bowdoin – or so I thought.

But then the very last day before graduation, Dick Steele, the Dean of Admissions and Financial Aid, called me in for some unknown reason. I was shitting bricks – was he going to tell me that I wouldn't receive my diploma? Had they made a mistake in
~~~~~~~~~~~~~~~~~~~~~~~~~~~~

my financial aid and I owed more? That would be a disaster, I had a big student loan hanging over my head as it was, and I didn't have any extra cash at all.

As I walked in for this meeting I couldn't help thinking about all these questions. I sat down quietly and nervously waited for the bad news. Dean Steele started the conversation by telling me that he recognized how some students struggled to afford a Bowdoin education even while working hard to achieve academic success.

What was he building up to? I nearly broke down even before he said anything else. I couldn't look at him in the eye for fear of
tears forming. He proceeded to say that the school rec
struggles and hardship, and that an anonymous alu
generously covered my entire Perkins Loan. I was, to s
stunned – or to use a really big word, quite utterly fla

As I lined up to receive my diploma on a most gorg
day of May 27th, pollen attacked my allergies and I ha
and blow my nose walking down to sit in the front ro
couldn't process my Bowdoin experience. As I sat
listening to the speeches, I had flashbacks to the day
ago when Karen enthusiastically welcomed me to campus. I felt the depth of my relationship with all the male friends who'd had my back – not to mention the various heartaches, romances, depression unto near suicide. And then the financial surprise from Dick Steele.

In short, I finished college with many mixed emotions. I'd finished up at Bowdoin and proven to myself and my parents that I could make it through a high-quality American education. I had made some true friendships that would endure. I knew where I was going next – and it seemed that I was in love.

Arkady had secured a job in New York City as a first-year investment banker. As expected, we hadn't talked about our future, but we both kind of assumed that we would continue being together. Princeton and New York after all were quite close so we'd see each other, right?

And then we graduated and Ark went off to the Big Apple to start his job. And … I did a strange thing. I decided for the first time really in my life to take some time off and do nothing, just hang out at home and chill. I wanted to start the next step in my education feeling fresh, perhaps this time on a better note, at Princeton.

I was actually amazed that I could just hang out at home for a couple months that summer. Somehow something inside me had changed through graduating from Bowdoin. And my parents related to me differently also. My dad especially began to see me in a new light – as someone who could actually get out there in this new culture and succeed, perhaps even at high levels. He felt very proud of me – and he also gave me a few lectures about staying focused, not getting caught in any romantic involvements that would lead to pregnancy and ruin my future … and so forth.

Then it was August, it was time to leave Lawrence again. I drove my trusty old Jeep Grand Cherokee down to New Jersey, filled with all my school supplies for grad school. My parents came down too, in their beat-up minivan. They were so excited to see the beautiful Princeton campus as they realized their daughter was actually going to be doing something with her life beyond bagging groceries or cleaning houses or delivering mail.

The drive down felt magical. Even the scenery on both sides of the NJ Transit felt like heaven. And when we got to campus, the noble stone-castle buildings with their gothic architectural details and the lush green trees and lawns and golf course – it definitely created the perfect idyllic backdrop. Princeton does have the loveliest and most beautiful campus.

When my parents walked around – well I'd never seen them smile like that, with such pure happiness. They saw their daughter moving up in society and assimilating in ways that they never imagined possible when we first came to this country. They were also happy to see me feeling upbeat and at ease for the first time since I went off to college.

We walked around campus and soaked in what refugees often feel when arriving in a new safe place – like being immersed in a dream. This was such a proud moment for my parents because this wasn't a dream – it was quite real. How had I gone in just two decades from being hopelessly adrift on a floundering boat and then pillaged and ravaged by Thai pirates, to being on this idyllic campus where the cream of the American crop ends up?

For my parents, being able to study on a full two-year scholarship at Princeton was also a pure blessing. We had survived without hardly any food or shelter, and then immigrated to a country that looked at us as 'aliens' – we'd survived all the hate and nonstop racism. Struggling in America along with all the other lower-class outcasts of society, we'd simply had to accept and deal with poverty and mistreatment.

Life for immigrants or people of color often was not fair at all. So yes, I was remarkably fortunate to be here at Princeton. I relished the beauty of the campus, the cleanliness and the greenery, and the excitement I was feeling about being able to study here – and at least pretend that I was a brilliant intellectual.

Meanwhile I was waiting for my parents to leave so that Arkady could come down from New York to visit. At that time none of our parents knew that we were dating, they still thought we were just good-buddy friends. Ark didn't want to take the chance of finding out what his parents would think about him dating a non-Russian and non-Jewish person. He'd already experienced his parents' pain when his brother married a non-Jewish Russian woman – he didn't want to put his parents through that pain again.

My mom and dad were similar. They were always worried that I'd ruin my professional aspirations by dating before I was thirty and a success in something. Like I said, they wanted me to focus totally on myself, my studies and my career. So … I never said anything to them about my private life. I knew they would instantly reject my deepening relationship with Arkady. So again, my natural reflex to be transparent got bent out of shape by my not wanting to upset people.

Right after they'd gone back to Boston, Arkady came down on the New Jersey Transit from Penn Station, and I drove out to pick him up at Princeton Junction. I remember that day being very passionate, hugging each other in this new situation after many weeks apart. It was super hot and muggy, and so was the sex. We loved getting together over the next months– but we never really talked about whether we would stay together. We just kept joining up each weekend, first at Princeton, then in New York, then at Princeton again.

But really, underneath my happy facade, I found that I mostly felt like an impostor at Princeton. For the first time ever, I was where I really wanted to be. I wanted to have a wonderful college experience, feel fully accepted for who I truly was, meet people whom I could connect with, and learn exciting new things. But almost from the first week of classes, I felt insecure with my intellect. I was cognizant that I was behind the other students in the grad program in terms of experience, social skills and intellect.

Attending graduate school at Princeton made me feel an insecurity that still looms over me. And quite soon this insecurity of not being smart or suave enough was solidified when some of my classmates actually lobbied for the school to not accept individuals like myself in their midst. They said I was too young, too immature, too inexperienced.

Of course in some ways they were mostly correct. I was quite in awe of my classmates' impressive experience, intellectual curiosity and their seemingly-innate ability to speak so eloquently. They had in abundance everything that I lacked, or thought I lacked – therefore I felt seriously inadequate. I couldn't write as well as they could. I could barely speak without making grammatical mistakes – and this was evident every time I opened my mouth.

But always before in school, I could overcome my academic failings with hard work. Perseverance and tenacity. That basic migrant struggle-and-survive attitude was my modus operandi, it had been ingrained into me literally from birth. But at Princeton I was forced to go one step further to survive – I had to develop what I came to call my impostor syndrome.

The reality was that I could no longer believe in and rely on just hard work. I had to put on a superior image where I pretended to be smarter and cooler than I actually was. And I admit, ever since then all of my successes have been overshadowed by the feeling that one disastrous day, people would realize that I'm simply an impostor.

But Princeton wasn't all bad by any means. My grumbling insecurities were often muted by an overwhelming joy of meeting people who actually did accept me. They weren't necessarily people of color, or poor, or recent immigrants. Yes, I had a few similar-background friends in the program who always had my back and understood me. With them I enjoyed a quiet mutual acceptance that reminded me of comradery back in high school where we gave dap to signify solidarity. And there were also some students I got close with at Princeton who were of completely differing backgrounds but treated me as an equal.

I recall one time meeting a woman standing in line next to me outside a stone-castle building with a large cannon in front. We were waiting in line to receive some sort of computer service. I introduced myself, "Mai, like tie MY shoe," and she introduced herself as Mehvesh. I had her repeat her name because I couldn't quite catch the pronunciation.

Mehvesh spoke with a slight British accent of some sort, it sounded mostly British to me. She spoke with all the confidence and smoothness that I lacked. I was mesmerized by how she could string words together so beautifully, as though she'd spent hours beforehand thinking about what to say.

She told me that before coming to Princeton she'd studied at the London School of Economics. As she was speaking I found myself thinking of Naeem, even before she told me she was from Pakistan. Something between me and Mehvesh connected – but it definitely wasn't our backgrounds. She was from a wealthy family, she was a first-class world debater, beautiful, eloquent and well-groomed from an early age.

Everything came so fluidly and easily for Mehvesh, from her speech to her grace to her ability to grasp esoteric concepts with full confidence. I on the other hand was a Mekong boat-person who could seldom utter the correct words needed to engage in intellectual grad-school conversations. I often walked away when Mehvesh and a group of our classmates masturbated over ideological concepts that honestly didn't have any particular impact on my life or the lives of others like myself. Perhaps yes, I'm at heart just a simpleton without depth.

But at other times Mehvesh and I could stay up all night talking one-on-one about nothing of academic or political importance – things like life, love, pain, trust, faith. Not necessarily conversations that would interest the well-pedigreed, but conversations flowing from our hearts that broke down or rather melted barriers.

The more time I spent with Mehvesh, the more I felt like I was hanging out with Naeem. They both had an uncanny similarity in personalities, interests and idiosyncrasies. I often secretly found myself imagining them together – how perfect a union it would be. But although I enjoyed being around Mehvesh, I wondered what it was about me that interested her. Perhaps my comparative simplicity allowed her to be safe and vulnerable around me.

Chapter Eleven

~~~~~~~~~~~~~~~~~~~~~~~~~~~~~~

Grad school was very different than college, both in my mind and in my heart. Back at Bowdoin I can now see that my myopic view of the world had limited me from becoming friends with people who were dissimilar to me, except when I was in Paris. At Bowdoin I stayed inside a close circle of friends who were racially, culturally and socio-economically different from the mainstream 'Bowdoin kids'.

But then in grad school I was thankfully a bit more mature, and my experiences in Paris had quite deeply changed me – to where I now allowed my circle of friends to expand naturally beyond my old comfort zone, regardless of how uncomfortable that expansion might initially feel. I'd always loved hiking and climbing, and somewhat naively climbing up that Princeton ivory tower and social ladder felt metaphorically equivalent. Because of a tremendous fear of heights, I delighted in the climb upward – but this was always accompanied by my fear of getting up much higher than I'd ever been before.

I definitely relished the new feeling of being at least somewhat included in high academic society. But as my connections expanded and I broke through more social barriers, I regularly got hit with the panic of fearing I'd climbed too high – and would suddenly topple and fall. I guess I was feeling social vertigo.
~~~~~~~~~~~~~~~~~~~~~~~~~~~~~~

As I mentioned, I have always naturally gravitated toward friends and groups that felt familiar in one way or another. As I think about this, I realize I didn't actively seek out those friendships. I was just being narrow-minded and not looking beyond my habitual horizon. But in my grad program at Princeton, I risked stepping out in the hope of getting to know more of my classmates a bit better – but in that rarified atmosphere quite a number of my fellow classmates made it clear that as far as they were concerned, I just didn't belong.

Once that was made clear to me, I avoided trying to relate with individuals who hung out in the group that subtly made it more than clear, through their slight snubs, that they didn't want me in their circle or our program or in the grad school at all. My reaction of uncertainty and fear and hurt, along with various misunderstandings and misconceptions, led me to avoid everyone associated with this rejecting group of classmates.

However, one of these people was KG, who as it turned out is one of the most fabulous persons I know. She was able to relate comfortably in all groups because she holds an open mind and heart for all the struggles happening around the world. But only by rooming with her during my second year at Princeton did I allow myself to see beyond my fears and stereotypes.

So – what did some of my classmates do toward me at Princeton that upset me and has negatively affected me to this day? Most of the graduate classes at SPIA were known to be very tight and supportive groups – but our class was different, in that some of my classmates quite openly began expressing their firm objection to having someone like me in their grad program.

From my current perspective I honestly don't think this had anything to do with my skin color or my socio-economic background. Their rejecting attitude toward me might appear racially biased – but what seemed to upset these students wasn't my color. It was that they thought younger students like me weren't intellectual enough or experienced enough to participate in their midst. And somehow I was an easy target compared to my other fellow classmates who also had limited work experience.

I had already sensed that I was somewhat out of place on some levels due to my inexperience in real-world situations. It's true, I didn't have very much experience at an office job compared with others in my class, who were older and therefore had 'been around' more than I had. Also there was the factor of my not being able to communicate with the air of confidence and intelligence that most of my classmates exhibited.

These critical classmates didn't know, because I couldn't articulate my inner thoughts and feelings, that in many ways I saw the world with quite a deep understanding because of my life history. They didn't know that I'd been born into and endured starvation and violence, that I'd experienced first-hand America's own poverty-ridden immigrant situation, or ridden a motorbike throughout south Vietnam interviewing executives, local government officials and villagers regarding the impact of multinationals on their society.

Regardless or perhaps because of my lack of sharing at this personal level, a group of my classmates did not want me there and they quite soon formally expressed their objection to the administration. But John, the Dean of Admissions, came to my defense and squashed all efforts to change admission policy to keep people like me out of the program.

John overtly emailed the entire school explaining the school's admission policy, emphasizing his stance that meaningful and valuable experience comes in many different forms. So I was defended – but I still felt the sting of that group of mostly white male classmates who thought that the school had made a mistake in accepting someone … like me.

Unfortunately that unexpected disruption of our class harmony further cemented my feeling that I would always be on the periphery of American society – and it further provoked what I call my impostor syndrome. Being told in no uncertain terms by fellow classmates that I didn't belong where I was, this felt like salt thrown on an open wound, especially following similar feelings back at Bowdoin. Somehow I'd expected that my experience at Princeton would be different.

Ever since, I've pondered why that group of supposedly open-minded liberal classmates felt the urgent need or desire to loudly voice their dislike of another classmate's presence. I always wondered why my very presence was seen as inhibiting these classmates from having the expected and intended experience they so hoped for at Princeton.

Honestly, for a whole group of my classmates to consume themselves for weeks with whether a fellow classmate deserved to belong to their group – it seemed to me that this defeated the whole purpose of their being in a grad school with a mission to fight bigotry and injustice in the world. They seemed to be acting out an example of the very problem they said they were committed to solving. This was for me perplexing, to say the least.

Looking objectively back, it does seem that I deserved to be in that grad program at Princeton, at least just as much as my fellow classmates did. I didn't really defend myself at all at the time, but I can see now that I should never have allowed others to diminish my sense of self-worth – but the whole thing was such an unexpected shock to me. I again felt out of place – but this time it wasn't about my race or where I came from. It was very much an old-fashioned caste thing, reminding me of the Boston Brahmins, that elite upper-class clique who judged everyone based on specific pre-established characteristics that qualified the privileged few to belong to their special group. I was simply not qualified in their eyes, even if the Princeton admissions team thought I was.

I wished I'd never been forced to deal with this type of insecurity and rejection, but that's just how my life unfolded, even at Princeton. For better or for worse, such encounters had shaped me ever since having to flee my homeland and migrate to America. But as usual I did my best to carry on. Despite my intellectual insecurities and communication challenges, I did all I could to hang in and work hard and continue with my grad-school studies. I compartmentalized and blocked my hurt feelings, and focused intently on learning. I was being given a unique opportunity, so why not see it through?

At Princeton I met a wonderful friend named Ajai, who would remain close for the duration. Late at night he'd talk all of this over with me, and point out that opportunity and privilege came to people mostly through pure luck. Being born into a privileged life, with all sorts of open doors and resources readily available – that was nothing more than pure good fortune. Ajai believed that we don't get to choose our family or environment, but we do have the opportunity to act and change our future.

And I was determined to change mine, and I actually somehow did very well at Princeton academically. I didn't allow my internal struggles to slow me down. I was excited to learn and thrive, in my own way. However, I never thought that my academic successes ensued from natural intelligence, but rather stemmed from my family example and cultural inheritance of total devotion to non-stop hard work and tough determination. I didn't necessarily disagree with my overly-critical classmates – I didn't think I was as smart as they were. But I was not going to admit defeat.

In that lofty Princeton environment, I was thankful that at Bowdoin I'd decided to tackle my fear of writing essays by taking courses that required one paper after another. Grad school was simply a continuation of that. And because in high school I'd learned how to type very fast, in college I could type verbatim what the professor was saying, capturing a two-hour lecture word by word. I sometimes shared an entire transcription of notes with classmates.

In my first year I signed up for very difficult 'C-track' Econ and Stats classes, with a brave small group of other classmates that happened to include Mehvesh and Ajai. We really got our asses kicked, but we also had one hell of a good time studying together through many late nights.

Those upper-level classes were so very hard, and I wondered many years later why I put myself through all that stress when overall it really didn't make a difference in my life. I guess I felt that if I didn't struggle or push myself, I didn't deserve to be there.

It was probably my own way to prove my worth and place. This compulsion to torture and push myself to the limit has certainly contributed to my success, but it's had detrimental effects on my health and relationships.

It's quite fascinating to observe how raising our social and economic position shifts our priorities, struggles, and worries – we move from fixating on third-world necessities such as food and safety and shelter, to first-world considerations like developing more adequate intellectual capabilities and fitting into select groups. I definitely saw this change in myself.

From birth up through high school, everything for me had been about making sure we had enough of the basics, and trying to stay safe in a tough neighborhood. Then in college and grad school, my classmates were of an entirely different order, and things I'd never worried about before, like my looks and intellectual capacity and communication skills, became front and center.

After experiencing social mobility from the very bottom of the totem pole, step by step to a much higher altitude, I came to realize through observing my classmates that regardless of where they were placed on that totem pole, there seemed to always be considerable stress and worry affecting all of us both mentally and emotionally – and at deeper existential levels as well.

Arkady often reminded me that "Your attitude, not your aptitude, will determine your altitude." That's of course mostly true, and I constantly struggled to break free from attitudes I'd inherited from my background that held me back. But I also had to face head-on, over and over again, that the world simply isn't a fair playing field. People born in high places often squander their good luck, while people born low down within the world's subtle caste system, even in America, must deal with their birth position as best they can.

Here's one more thought about my particular class at Princeton. As I mentioned, most class cohorts in our grad program were known to grow very close as a group. The classers both above us and below mine were really tight. The class below us was so close that they even went on vacations together, they did almost everything as a group, they were as tight knit as a woven blanket.

If I had gone out into the world after Bowdoin, and come a year later to Princeton, I would have been with this tight-knit class and my future journey would have been very different. But of course I wouldn't change how that all went, because even as I utter these words I realize that if I'd been in a different class at Princeton, I wouldn't have met Mehvesh, Ajai, Reggie, Rodney, KG, and many other long-lasting friends.

But our class for some reason just didn't seem to gel and bond as a group. But we appear to be more cohesive now, especially with our WhatsApp group. Perhaps maturity and age have changed people. Even with our WhatsApp group I often don't feel a sense of belonging – but I accept that this is possibly all in my head. No one makes me feel this way today.

Chapter Twelve

~~~~~~~~~~~~~~~~~~~~~~~~~~~~~~

Like back at Bowdoin, I often escaped from Princeton during the weekends, to reset my mind and be with a group of friends who openly welcomed me as one of their own. But now, rather than going home to family and high-school friends as I did at Bowdoin, I traveled to NYC to be with Arkady and my group of friends who had moved there after college.

In contrast to my Princeton classmates, in New York I felt zero pressure to be something I wasn't. Nor was I expected to always speak intelligently, eloquently or confidently. So – every weekend, I jumped on the New Jersey Transit to Penn Station. During the fifty-minute-or-so train ride, I often looked out the window and stared out into the world passing by. Somehow that felt relaxing and offered me a few special moments of solace, like my time in Paris when I would sit on a bench watching random people passing by me.

I felt both alone and also content, temporarily away from all of my work, out of reach from the usual noise of my life. I was just with me, and free to be me. It was perhaps the solitude described in Jean-Jacque Rousseau's *L'esprit de Solitude.* And then when I got into New York I felt like Carrie Bradshaw in *Sex in the City* – ready to explore, to see Arkady, to go to jazz clubs, explore the food culture and live for yet another weekend on top of the world
~~~~~~~~~~~~~~~~~~~~~~~~~~~~~~

– I was in my early 20s in the big city and New York was fabulous, I loved everything about it.

For both me and Ark, this city situation was beyond our dreams, being entirely away from our parents and school environments. We weren't formally together, as we'd both already agreed that we would part ways as a romantic duo after Bowdoin. More to the point, we just never broached the conversation about whether to remain together. It seemed that we just happened to continue to hang out and spend our free time exploring the Big Apple, growing into adult individuals beyond the bounds of parental expectations or college social bubbles.

In New York, Ark and I effortlessly learned to indulge fully in sensory experiences and physical delights. Arkady took me to fancy restaurants like *Asia de Cuba* and *Indochin*e. He was now an investment banker after all, he had money and he wanted us to experience the life we'd never had before. What an ongoing feast of the senses!

At these fun and fancy places we usually joined up with our other friends, who happened to be mostly Pakistanis. Enjoying this Empire state of mind came with no guilt, at least for me – which allowed me to freely indulge in everything around me. I could temporarily forget that I had parents who were still struggling financially, I forgot that I was a lowly refugee. I think it was only during those weekends in NYC that those forever-looping thoughts disappeared. I think that during those weekends, Ark and I attained true happiness together.

Then when I came back to Princeton, I came back into reality. I would start worrying again about my parents' financial situation, brainstorming to find new ways to help them by sending money home. Often this meant that I took out loans, since I didn't have any extra cash on my own – and I later would manage to pay off those loans myself.

When I saw Mehvesh I would tell her about my time with my Pakistani friends, about our going out to restaurants and enjoying plays. Then one weekend I impulsively invited her to come with me on my next trip. I happily introduced her to a small group of my friends at a cozy restaurant – Arkady and Naeem, several people from Pakistan and a Caucasian woman. There was magic in the air that evening. We shared constant laughter all evening, talking about the silliest things like eating the Pakistani delicacy of chopped goat testicles which is called *kata-kat*.

After dinner we went for a walk to get some *chai*. I could tell that Naeem, meeting Mehvesh for the first time, was completely smitten. He followed her around like a puppy on our walk. Mehvesh saw someone she knew in a store and when she walked in to say hi, Naeem followed her while the rest of us stood outside. He was completely taken by Mehvesh and I was secretly ecstatic. Something special happened that evening while we were talking about goat testicles and then sipping tea. I had realized my secret desire to bring Mehvesh and Naeem together – and it all happened so naturally.

But in my own romantic involvement with Arkady, one thing I continued to realize during that phase of our relationship was that I still didn't feel that I was anything special to him. Ark was certainly no Cary Grant sweeping me off my feet on the bateau-mouche – but I reminded myself that practicality in a relationship was more important than silly romance. Still, I'd too often in the last five years seen him do special things for other girlfriends. I'd been with him when he wanted to make his first Valentine's Day with his Bulgarian girlfriend super special by engraving *Obicham Te* (I love you) on a pendant. I had also helped him get two dozen long-stem roses for his Russian girlfriend when he was in London and she was back home in Boston.

However, when it came to his relating with me, I was just his best friend with whom he happened to be sexually intimate. He never did hardly anything at all for any of my birthdays, for Valentine's Day, or other special occasions. He of course did take me out to really nice dinners and shows in New York when I visited him, he would cover my costs. And he was the wonderful guy who'd slept on my hardwood floor for many nights while I was immobile and ill back in college. But he wasn't going to give me the stomach-flutter-with-butterflies romance that I yearned for.

Probably Ark was everyone else's Cary Grant – a tall dark handsome banker, seeming quite mysterious and intriguing because he never really shared what he deeply felt or thought. And of course he didn't realize how much I wanted to feel with him that same mind-blowing loverly feeling that I'd experienced kissing Ben in moonlight alongside the Seine.

I wanted that with Arkady but it just wasn't there – and I'd wonder if we were together simply because it was comfortable? More and more I began to feel frustrated. Even though externally things seemed just fine, I started to sense that it was time for us to discuss whether we should finally part ways – but whenever I brought up the subject he would get upset. He'd tell me he loved me but he wouldn't talk about us as a couple, at least not in any deep, meaningful way.

And so I went up to NYC less often as my first year at Princeton continued. I was beginning to think more seriously that I was overdo to separate from him. In my mind I felt more and more detached from him. I told myself that I was now in grad school, living in a new environment – and maybe I should leave my old life behind and start fresh with someone new.

Then my grad-school friend Reggie introduced me to his friend at Yale Law. We connected on a cerebral level and that had never happened before – but there was definitely quite a strong attraction. After spending an enjoyable day with this gentleman, he asked me to come visit him at Yale. I hesitated, as I was still technically with Arkady. My mind said no but my heart said go. I was craving for that carefree feeling of newness – so I went.

I had the best time exploring Yale with him. I felt truly happy. Then he came to visit me a few weeks later at Princeton and we enjoyed each other's company even more. Things progressed after dinner one evening, he asked if I would consider being with him. My heart wanted to say yes, that special feeling was so strong. But my mind said … no. While I'd never felt that special with Arkady, I just couldn't walk away and break his heart.

I softly rejected this person's kind and loving request. We hugged each other tightly for a long time, and then wished each other a wonderful future before he drove back to Yale. Arkady and I continued as we had before, but ending many weekends with bitter feelings. I began spending more weekend time at Princeton, diving deeper into my studies.

Meanwhile Naeem was falling more for Mehvesh and vice versa, and I was often their secret messenger. Naeem was a hopeless romantic and if he learned that Mehvesh wanted or needed something, anything at all, he would secretly coordinate with me to help her get what she desired, but without ever revealing to her his involvement.

I found myself living vicariously through their courting because I'd never experienced that level of courtship myself. But I told myself, why should I care so much about romance? I now had everything I needed to live more comfortably than I ever had before. I told myself that I should develop a pragmatic approach to love – and enjoy my present situation in life. I was at one of the top institutions in the country, my education costs and living expenses were all being covered, I was constantly surrounded by brilliant people, plus eating wonderful meals and partying in NYC whenever I wanted to.

And it was true – I was hanging with someone who was a good and caring person. In my also yearning for romance, was I asking life for too much? My parents had never celebrated special occasions – for them the dimension of romance was considered unimportant. As long as you had each other and treated each other with respect, that was considered by them a good relationship. Romance was an indulgent first-world privilege.

But whether or not it was a pointless privilege, I still very deeply wanted to be romanced. I'd felt its magic sporadically before – and it was a delicious liberating feeling that took me off and away from mundane reality. I loved that in-love feeling! And so yes, I still dreamed that one day I'd be granted that kind of love.

Dreams are meant to be just dreams – but at Princeton I started to drift away from remaining grounded in my past, my values, my culture and my whole refugee experience. Living in Princeton with all its fairy-tale castles and lofty luxurious possibilities seemed to stimulate and reinforce a liberated feeling growing inside me. I began to ask myself, hey – maybe romance isn't just a wasteful luxury reserved for the privileged few. Maybe it's a human birthright that all of us should be able to experience in our lives – really!

In the midst of such swirling ideas and emotions, my second semester at Princeton ended. I applied for and was offered an interesting internship at the United Nations Development Program which would take me off to Bangkok for the summer. I was beyond thrilled to be able to return to Southeast Asia. I called my parents in excitement – but they reacted to my plans with overt anger and also emotional pain.

Why? Because they still hated Thailand with a passion on account of how terribly we'd been mistreated when escaping from Vietnam. After over twenty years, they still carried such a hot reactive charge against anything Thai-related. They actually ordered me not to accept the internship, and when I went against their orders they were terribly upset – outraged when I continued with plans to fly to Bangkok.

They complained that their eldest child never obeyed them, that I was always defying all their guidance, values and expectations – but this in reality wasn't fair or true. After all, I never got pregnant as a teen, I never joined a gang, I never used drugs or did anything that they would disapprove of. Yes, I spoke my mind and did what

I thought was best. And damnit, in this case going to Thailand was important to my career, I needed the experience – and also, I so very much wanted to be back in Southeast Asia.

I knew also that it would be good to take a break from Arkady. I felt stagnated, confused and frustrated with our relationship at that point. It didn't seem to be evolving, it wasn't moving forward like I yearned for it to. We superficially talked about my coming trip to Thailand, and the unspoken assumption was that while I was gone we'd stay together, and speak occasionally on the phone. And as was Ark's habit, there was no special goodbye event before I left.

Chapter Thirteen

~~~~~~~~~~~~~~~~~~~~~~~~~~~~~~

Arriving in Bangkok felt surreal. It was hot, muggy and tropical – and once again, arriving in that part of the world immediately made me feel like I belonged. It felt so natural, I looked like everyone around me. In the city I was often asked where I was from, and if I said America they would say, "No, no. Where are you really from?"

But if I then told them that I'm Vietnamese, they would look down on me. Thais were considered better off than all the other Southeast Asian countries – wealthier, prettier, and wise enough to have avoided the war. But regardless, I was feeling like I was in heaven, back home in the motherland and eagerly relating with the local people, food and weather.

During my first week in Thailand I was temporarily housed in an apartment while I coordinated with the United Nations office in Bangkok. I remember that the rooms were walled with teak wood and teak furniture. With no air conditioner and the region's usual high humidity, it felt like being back in Vietnam with my grandparents – except that I was in a giant city.

Because I was a young Vietnamese woman, I didn't feel completely safe in the city. The reality was that there were a lot of sex traffickers and I carried my parents' biggest fear that I would disappear or be violated by the same type of people who'd violated women on my boat and wanted to chop off my ears. So I
~~~~~~~~~~~~~~~~~~~~~~~~~~~~~~

was very careful while in Bangkok, although the chances of something bad happening to me were probably quite low.

When I went to the UN building I sat at my assigned desk in awe and looked around with pure happiness. I soon met my boss who joyfully welcomed me to Bangkok, explaining how the office functioned and my stated goals for the summer as a student intern. Curiously he also highly recommended, for out-of-office excursions, that I see certain shows in the city – shows he said I would never see anywhere else in the world – but at the time I didn't quite understand what he was suggesting.

Feeling enthusiastic to get started, I met the staff. A number of them were Thai and I got on perfectly well with them. The Thai people were quite nice to me, and during my time there I didn't encounter the type of Thai people that my parents had encountered – except on one occasion when a taxicab driver purposely drove in the opposite direction of where I was supposed to go. Realizing something was wrong, I asked the driver to stop – but he refused. I screamed in Thai for him to stop but that didn't help. Thank goodness for congested traffic which gave me a chance to jump out. I had a flash of my parents' worst nightmare but I wasn't necessarily rattled by this event. I just hailed another taxi and continued to my destination.

I explored Bangkok as much as I could on my very small intern stipend for the summer. I didn't quite know how I'd be able to rent a place, eat, and explore – but when I mentioned to a colleague that I had to find a very inexpensive but also safe apartment, he immediately said he was living in a large apartment and offered me a room rent free. He explained that he usually was traveling and wasn't home much, and he thought the space should be used.

I was a bit hesitant, as he was a single man whom I barely knew. But when I asked around, everyone said that he was a good guy, so I gave it a try. I soon moved into a gorgeous building on the bank of the Chao Praya River. The view, merging the ancient cultural east with glass-and-steel modernism, was breathtaking from the apartment balcony. As the sun set, the city lit up with shadows of pagodas and temples brushing alongside the high-rise buildings of Bangkok. I felt that I could readily live in this region of the world and be happy. I felt like I fit in – except for my being Vietnamese.

As long as I didn't share where I was really from, people weren't prejudiced against me. I learned basic Thai and I could count to a hundred really fast because their numbering system is similar to Vietnamese. This allowed me to negotiate when out shopping at the market, and ordering food on the street. I found their street food was to die for, if your stomach could handle it. I devoured the food and savored the spiciness.

In the mornings when I stepped out, Bangkok was peaceful with many Buddhist novices and monks walking around in their orange robes. After a few minutes of walking in the humidity, I would be drenched in sweat from the monsoon heat. All around were tropical plants and beautiful orchids in hanging pots, with their roots exposed to absorb the moisture in the air. Orchids became my favorite flowers, I couldn't take my eyes off them. They were everywhere, lining buildings and hanging from palm trees.

More and more as the days and nights went by, I felt like I belonged here. I didn't stand out in the crowd, I blended in – and at that time in my life that felt like a very good thing. I remember how many years later, I gave my daughter a card I'd drawn for her first day of kindergarten. It had multiple tulips which were all the same color, except for one that was different – and I wrote, "Stand out amongst the crowd." But while I was living in Bangkok that summer, after years of painful standing-out experiences in America, I was definitely wanting to blend in – and so I did.

Sometimes I found myself wishing Arkady could be here so that we could explore this part of the world together – but I didn't think he'd be able to handle it, I feared that he was too delicate to travel to second and third world countries, as we called them back then. Today we call them developing and middle-income countries. But in contrast to Ark, their rawness definitely appealed to me.

Like one of my favorite explorers, Anthony Bourdain, I liked to venture as far as I safely could into the vivid human vibrancy of these cultures. I had the time of my life during that summer. And, mostly through my U.N. work, I met people from all around the world. In addition to work encounters, we would meet up for dinners and weekend excursions. We traveled north to Chiang Mai, and also south.

On my birthday a small group of us took a bus south and then a boat over to a Thai island called Koh Chang or the elephant island, which still remains pristine and untouched by modern development. Being on that island felt like being in the movie *The Beach* with Leonardo DiCaprio. We arrived and took off in a small bus through a dense green jungle with remote villages here and there, along our way to a small village of just a few huts located on a most beautiful tropical beach where we were totally away from civilization.

I couldn't believe that I was here with friends for my birthday, it was just so special. A friend and I decided to treat ourselves to a massage on the beach which was interesting to say the least, and I wasn't quite sure if I should enjoy it or not.

We walked into a hut on the beach with a palm-leaf roof and three walls, the fourth open to the sea. We were asked to take everything off except for our underwear. We wrapped ourselves in towels and proceeded to lie face down. The ocean breeze came sweeping into the hut and cooled my face. Oil was poured on my back and I felt my muscles being rubbed gently but firmly. All my thoughts disappeared and my mind wandered … then my backside was completed and I was nudged to turn over.

The masseuse pulled down my towel to expose my small breasts with their large nipples. My friend seemed totally comfortable being exposed like this because in her native country she was accustomed to Swedish baths and being naked around others. Okay, fine, I decided, and allowed the masseuse to continue. She massaged my neck and shoulders. That felt good. Then came my arms and stomach.

And then I felt an odd sensation that usually occurs only when I'm intimate with a man – because the masseuse was now massaging my nipples, lathered in oil. Hmmm. Was it okay to feel this way? Am I paying for sexual favors? I looked over and my friend was receiving the same treatment. I relaxed and allowed the masseuse to continue. Finishing with my nipples, she moved down to my legs and toes. That was definitely a nice birthday gift to myself.

The rest of the time we sat on the beach and soaked in the sun and warmth, drank Chang Beer, and wandered the shore with absolutely no thoughts of work, life, or pressure on our minds. I usually detest beaches but that weekend I loved the beach. I was free – and felt even freer when we dared each other to skinny dip in the ocean in the dark.

On an island densely covered in jungle and no light except for the moon and lights from our hut, the beach was quite dark. The sound of the waves crashing on the beach was so soothing. We stood there laughing and wondering if we'd dare strip and go naked into that ink-black water. I suddenly felt so nervy that I tore off my clothes and jumped into the ocean. And somehow … I felt a definite closure. Here I was in that same ocean where I'd started my long-ago journey to that terrible refugee camp in Thailand. I was now finally able to reconnect with the sea – and this time it was a vastly more positive experience.

Arkady didn't reach out to congratulate me during my birthday weekend – in fact he wouldn't have been able to, as I was on that remote island. But I thought of him and wanted to speak with him, so I purchased an international card to make a call from the island to NYC. I spoke to Ark briefly and he wished me happy birthday. But as usual he didn't say anything intimate or touching like I hoped he would.

Our conversation was neither exciting nor scintillating, and I had tears in my eyes when we hung up. I quickly wiped them away, not wanting my friends to see my sadness and ruin this marvelous weekend. But I felt more and more distant from Ark. In fact, as I returned to Bangkok after that idyllic island weekend, I felt so lonely and heartbroken that I wished I'd never fallen in love with him back at Bowdoin – and I also wished that we'd broken up right after graduation. Instead we were continuing in limbo, in a state of romantic nowhere.

But meanwhile I loved Bangkok and my work, and this solidified my interest in international development. During my assignment in Thailand I gathered data covering HIV/AIDS, child trafficking, and public-private partnership in developing countries. Doing this work felt so natural to me. And I also very much loved the Bangkok night life. I explored the markets and went out to bars after work.

One night I went out with my roommate who had just broken up with his girlfriend. We went out with a couple of people and danced at a bar. When we got home we somehow found ourselves kissing – but I thought of Ark during that intimate moment, and broke away. Awkwardness followed. I was thinking: will he kick me out now? But that didn't happen. He kindly allowed me to stay on in his apartment until I wrapped up my internship.

I shared with Arkady what had happened, I called him immediately after 'the kiss' incident – and he was immediately upset. He didn't want to talk further at all to me. So I hung up, feeling quite terrible that I'd hurt him – but I couldn't really understand why he was hurt. After all, he didn't show very much emotion toward me or commitment to our relationship. Had I hurt him as a friend or as a lover? Had I broken some unspoken trust with him? I attempted to mend the situation by deciding to send him flowers to his office – but that didn't seem to help.

The wild fast nightlife in Bangkok was the complete opposite of the serenity of the Bangkok mornings. The nights were bustling with colored lights and the sounds of people eating dinner outdoors on plastic chairs and tables, downing delicious street food. Vendors of all kinds lined the middle of the streets. I often haggled for the best-priced Thai silk. Since I could negotiate in Thai, if I came in low on an object, the vendor would ask me to step aside and wait if there were tourists standing around. When the coast was clear they would usually give me the price I'd asked for.

Meanwhile naked girls (often without a smile) were standing at the entrance doorways to the very same shows that my boss had suggested I go see. What a wild scene! One evening with some friends, I decided to try out the shows. We couldn't stop giggling with embarrassment as we watched mostly naked women performing various acts with their vaginas – shooting darts, smoking, pooping ping pong balls, and more. I had a full-frontal view, sitting at the edge of the stage. My boss had been right, I would never see this type of show anywhere else in the world.

I didn't want the summer to end but of course it did. Before I headed back, I went to the J&J Market to get a sizeable henna dragon tattoo covering my entire arm. I wanted to shock my dad and confirm for him that I was indeed the rebel daughter who defied him and went off to Thailand and got corrupted into inking my body. He abhorred tattoos, and my temporary henna looked so real. I flew back to Newark and took the train home to my parents' house in Lawrence.

My dad saw me and his neutral smile changed instantly upon seeing my tat. He was so upset that he went to his bedroom and remained there. I let him simmer for a bit, then I went in to let him know it was just a fake tattoo – but his facial expression didn't change. After my long trip home, I was exhausted and fell asleep on the couch. In the middle of my sleep, I felt a rough scrub moving up and down my arm. I woke up to my sister trying to remove the tattoo, at my father's directions.

When it was time to head back to grad school I packed my Jeep and drove down to Princeton. Over the phone I'd found out that Arkady had lost his job. He was stressed and busy looking for a new position. During the summer he and Naeem and another old Bowdoin friend had moved into an apartment together. He said he wanted me to come up to NYC to see him, so I unpacked and headed off to New York.

Arkady was returning from a trip to D.C. for an interview and I met him at Penn Station. We embraced, and did our usual thing – going out to eat, walking around, just spending time together. The date happened to be September 7th, 2001. I settled in a few days with Ark and Naeem because my classes didn't begin for a week or so. On Tuesday I wanted to go out and buy some new clothes – but I suddenly received a call from Naeem around 8:50 that morning pleading with me not to go out because an airliner had just crashed into the Twin Towers buildings. He told me to turn on the news – and right as we were talking the second plane hit the other tower.

We were in shock. We told each other to be safe and hung up. I woke up Arkady and told him the news. He was supposed to meet a Bowdoin alum at one of the towers just a few days earlier, but it had been rescheduled. That Bowdoin alum passed away that day. We were worried for all our friends at work around the city but we couldn't reach anyone, all the lines were down or overloaded.

During that day our Pakistani friends showed up at Naeem & Ark's apartment. We sat around in solidarity watching the news – it was all just so terrible and sad on so many levels. In our tiny apartment at Normandy Court on 96th and 3rd, the one thing about that day that sustained us was the support and friendship we felt, coming together like we did during that crisis.

Shortly after 9/11 a series of events left Naeem and his entire world shattered. He lost his job and his apartment was raided by the FBI. He was considered a terrorist suspect because of his name and date of birth coupled with some things he'd once said in a speech back in college. Meanwhile Ark had received an offer for a job in D.C., and he moved down there.

I remember my last time with Arkady in NYC before he moved to D.C. – it was the most beautiful autumn day ever. The air was fresh despite the recent events, the weather was unusually warm like an Indian summer, the foliage colorful in red, orange, and yellows. A gentle scented breeze engulfed us as we walked down Museum Row holding hands. But then Ark was gone from New York and that whole scene was all gone from my life. I occasionally went into the city for weekends but that era was over.

Chapter Fourteen

For my second year in grad school Mehvesh invited me to room with her, KG, and Q. I was close to Mehvesh and Q, and was friendly to KG but I hadn't gotten the chance to know her well in our first year. We hadn't had classes together and besides, she was friends with the group I suspected didn't want me there. But I was wrong about her, and during our second and final year at Princeton we bonded deeply.

I loved living with my new roommates. We had a nice arrangement, all four of us happily sharing in the cooking and cleaning responsibilities. But returning back from a class-sponsored trip to Senegal, I found out the hard way that I'd caught more than a few parasites. I'd stayed in a village where fifty years prior the villagers hadn't even worn clothes. So my adapting to the local culture and etiquette by eating with my hands from a shared platter had seemed entirely appropriate. I hadn't wanted to make my hosts feel uncomfortable by rejecting their sanitary levels, I wanted to respect their culture and way of living.

To put it more simply, what I ate there totally altered my bowel movements. I came back from the trip feeling seriously sick. It seemed that I'd caught every parasite possible, and that condition caused me to immediately run to the bathroom right after eating. When I left the bathroom the entire apartment would reek of sulfur.

My roommates sort of got used to this but it didn't stop them from screaming and yelling. We regularly had good laughs about the predicament. But I lost so much weight and was generally so weak that my parents drove down from Lawrence to Princeton just to cook me a pot of Vietnamese soup. It finally dawned on me that the feeling of love was unspoken in our family culture but that feeding me and doing other actions to support me, this was my parents' way of saying, "I love you."

As I started to recover from the parasite infection, I started to visit Arkady down in D.C. every other week. The distance required driving about two hours each way. He would occasionally come to visit me, but his work was demanding and often meant working during the weekend. We didn't argue or fight much during this time. I again made myself accept our relationship just as it was. He neither brought up the summer in Thailand nor the status of our relationship.

Who can say how much of my ongoing feelings of emotional distance from Arkady was being caused not by his feelings toward me, but by some early imprinted contractions inside my own heart caused by those early times. When Ark didn't show his love like my fantasy lover would, it'd bring up a lot of pain from not feeling special or not being that person he really wanted to be with – you know, the big-busted curvaceous Russian princess or something like that. But really, who can say where such long-term nagging feelings of loss originate from?

And of course Arkady had been seriously impacted by his own early childhood, that whole half-starved immigrant experience which he'd endured when he was quite young. We were both very close to our parents, and after arriving in America they still continued to pack all of their own emotional wounds, traumas and contractions. Why was Ark incapable of making me feel special, even on occasions such as birthdays, anniversaries, Christmas and Valentine's Day? I somehow completely failed to understand the psychological dynamics underlying our relationship.

And underlying all this – life in general continued to feel seriously different after 9/11 and all the giant shared trauma of shock, violation, tragedy, injustice and just plain existential fear. Everything I did for months felt so eerily sad and depressed in so many ways. The mood of the whole country and certainly our Princeton community was dark like my personal depression back at Bowdoin had been. There was such an oppressive emotional weight pressing down on all our chests. It was hard to take even an occasional good deep breath, let alone slip into giggle fits or indulge in any sensual pleasures.

And of course, because I'd been in New York City on that day, I couldn't shake off the trauma when I got out of the city and came back to campus. I remember a weird communal state of mind with everyone trying to comprehend what all this meant, while also being thankful that we were together and safe. And sadly, as more details were revealed in the news day by day, everything had pointed toward Pakistanis – and I had this foul premonition that something bad was going to happen to my Pakistani friends.

And of course that was what happened. Naeem, a brown man, had the same first and last name as a real terrorist on the FBI list, plus the same birthdate and country of origin – and that put him dangerously in America's anti-terrorist cross-hairs.

But my life at Princeton continued. I loved Princeton regardless of what had happened during my first year. I had friends, faculty, administration who welcomed me with open arms and who unknowingly helped me to mentally navigate Princeton's invisible social maze. As long as I had a few close friends I could make it through grad school.

My final semester was especially hard because I had to look for employment in the real world out there – and it dawned on me that I might have a problem finding a job. I mentioned my impostor syndrome earlier, of always feeling deep-down inadequate. No one made me feel this way, but even with my Princeton credentials I still felt like I didn't possess the necessary skill sets and natural talent to make my next step. I was just a very hard worker who persevered with significant tenacity to get over any barriers.

But I feared that that alone wouldn't be enough to get a good job in my field. I still struggled to communicate fluidly and to express myself with confidence. When I did express my thoughts they would either come out the wrong way, or lacking adequate power to affect change in opinion or feelings, whether it be one-on-one or an audience of a hundred. And now I would have to face dreaded interviews that would require me to pretend to exude the confidence and intellect that a Princeton grad should radiate. These interviews would certainly reveal the very thing that my own classmates had believed and fought to eradicate from their midst – my inadequate presence.

The Director of Career Services at Princeton was a woman named Ann. She and her husband helped my class practice with mock interviews. They videotaped our performances – and I totally bombed my mock interview. I could hardly believe how bad I looked and sounded on tape. I would never even hire myself based on those videotapes. Even today I'd never get a job based just on an interview alone. I've always gotten jobs because someone believed in me, took a risk with me or knew of my previous work.

I remember the very first interview of my life, which had been for admissions to UPenn. I didn't have the proper attire and I didn't prep. I had no idea what to expect – I just thought they wanted someone who was a good student, who had top grades in high school, which I did. I went in dressed like a person fresh off the boat. And I forgot to communicate anything about my significant contribution to my school, community and the city of Lawrence. All I told the interviewer was that I would study and work very hard at Penn. And … I wasn't accepted at Penn.

Now, faced with yet more interview trauma, I thought that maybe I should perhaps go for a PhD and remain a student forever. Being a student was relatively easy for me. I'd learned to navigate books and lectures quite well. If I tried and failed to do acceptable interviews for a job I feared that my imposter syndrome would be revealed and I'd finally get my immigrant ass kicked off of my overly-lofty posture in society.

But some part of me insisted that I take the great leap out of academia. I assumed I'd be the last person in my class to find a job so I got busy and applied everywhere, even to the CIA. I went very nervously to a CIA interview, where I was confronted with a question concerning America's global presence. I honestly said that I felt we shouldn't be in the war in Iraq.

The interviewer reacted with a tight expression that seemed to say, okay, this woman isn't gonna go anywhere, she should be defending American overseas policies. But that was how I truly felt, and I held my ground. This interview was the beginning of me daring to speak up and openly state my own opinions – and then accept whatever consequences came from letting my feelings roll spontaneously off my tongue.

So yeah, I obviously bombed that interview with the CIA and I also bombed many other interviews that spring before leaving Princeton – and as I'd feared, I ended up graduating without a job. But I had the summer months to delay the inevitable, as I was asked to join my friend Rodney to support and supervise the incoming summer cohort of Junior Summer Institute students at Princeton. That opportunity brightened my world more than I could have imagined.

This was basically the same program that I'd been lucky enough to participate in as a student several years earlier. These 33 students of color who were admitted, like myself, came during the summer before their senior year in college, for the two-month intensive program in public policy and international affairs. Rodney and I were program associates counseling and supporting them. For me it was a dream interim job!

Our role was to advise the students, organize social trips – and work with administration liaisons to make sure those students had the very best experience possible throughout that summer. While fulfilling our roles, Rodney and I became really close. Also during that summer Arkady came to visit – and in front of my students he would make comments about me that were very hurtful. At some point one of my students turned to me and asked: "Mai, how can you be with this guy?" There were a number of such instances where someone questioned why I was with Arkady – but I would always defend him even if his jokes or comments were actually hurtful and embarrassing.

That was just him. While growing up in his own intense immigrant situation he'd somehow developed a protective pretentious veneer, but underneath all of that was an unarticulated, carefully concealed and super-authentic human being loaded with empathy and compassion. Too often people don't see that big-hearted side of him because he habitually hides it – even from himself it seems.

My defense of Ark in situations where he seemed to be unkindly diminishing my self-worth stemmed from the fact that I knew him at deeper levels where he was the total opposite of a shallow arrogant person. Often that summer we did have good times together. Meanwhile I enjoyed my work with kids from so many different religions, nationalities and backgrounds. They were in many ways very similar to me with their struggles and experiences – and we could easily connect and enjoy a non-verbal solidarity of some sort.

I loved being with those students and I ended Princeton with a high bang. I also unexpectedly got hired for a job in Washington D.C. working as a policy research analyst within the Social Security Administration. Somehow as usual, despite all my worries, my life was continuing to unfurl.

PART SIX

~~~~~~~~~~~~~~~

Washington D.C./Africa
~~~~~~~~~~~~~~~

Chapter Fifteen

~~~~~~~~~~~~~~~~~~~~~~~~~~~~~~

I said goodbye to Princeton, drove home and hung out back in Lawrence for a week or so – and then got ready to move to D.C. to start my job in the Office of Policy at the Social Security Administration. Arkady offered me temporary quarters in his apartment until I could find a place for myself, and this offer took the stress off apartment hunting until I familiarized myself with the area.

I discovered that D.C. was diverse with eclectic ethnic cuisines from around the world with wide grid-like streets and unobstructed views of white marble monuments. It was the perfect place for me and Arkady because we loved living in a melting pot of all the cultures and foods of the world. But somehow, compared with New York, we didn't feel particularly at home in D.C. In our minds and hearts the place felt transient as a city, both for others and for ourselves. We wanted to settle more permanently closer to our families up in the Boston area.

Once I felt comfortable in my new job I started looking for an apartment – but I didn't really want to live all alone. And as it was autumn once again, when I went looking at apartments I felt a sense of loneliness and emptiness lurking all around me. Being able to stay with Arkady, knowing that I would come home to someone each evening, this gave me a much-needed sense of belonging and familiarity.
~~~~~~~~~~~~~~~~~~~~~~~~~~~~~~

All the constant change in my life from childhood through adulthood should have prepared me for yet another change – but somehow I was growing seriously tired of all the change. My temporary move into Ark's apartment step by step started to feel more like a permanent situation.

At that same time Ark's colleague Dave was crashing on the floor in the one-bedroom apartment – and all three of us began to enjoy quite good times together. Dave could certainly afford to rent his own apartment, but he enjoyed being with us and didn't mind sleeping on the floor. Dave and Ark were equity research analysts and they often worked around the clock. I often did too, so we were in similar work-buzz modes.

I had to explain to my parents why I'd moved in with Ark. Even while I was becoming more open and honest in most realms of my life, with my parents whom I never wanted to hurt or upset, I was still playing the game that Ark wasn't my boyfriend. My mom's devout Catholic beliefs and my parents' cultural traditionalism conflicted seriously with the whole idea of cohabitation before marriage, even with a 'friend'. My parents didn't want my aunt in Falls Church to know and word to get out that their daughter was, you know, loose.

But I was at least honest enough to inform them on the phone that I was sharing a D.C. apartment with a male friend – and as a result they didn't talk to me for a while. They said I had changed for the worse, that I wasn't the child I'd been all the way through high school. But I was determined to finally just be myself, regardless of what people thought.

I also found it fruitless to explain to my parents that living with Ark helped me mentally and emotionally, not to mention physically. Knowing that my parents weren't being supportive was hard for me, I hated not telling them the whole truth – that Arkady and I were basically a couple. And this somehow made me unable to fully embrace my love relationship.

Every time Arkady and I were intimate I got hit afterward with a mess of Catholic guilt feelings. I admit that I never quite broke free from that, I never felt comfortable with my relationship because I felt like I was living in sin. Like some of my gay friends, it seemed that I couldn't come out and say to the world that Ark was my boyfriend, that we were a couple.

And of course as usual, I didn't know what he was really feeling. I did know that his parents felt basically the same as my parents did. Arkady and I had been together for years, we'd gone through tough times and good times. But our parents knew nothing of this, and I was confused – should we just continue living at this uncertain level of togetherness?

Ark wasn't a practicing Jew but he strongly felt his overall Jewish identity – and he didn't want to commit to me because I wasn't the kind of woman his parents wanted him to marry. They wanted him to marry a Russian Jewish woman and like me, he always wanted to please his parents. He talked to them almost every day, usually when I wasn't around. His brother had married outside the family faith, and his parents hadn't even been invited to the wedding. That slight was always in the back of Arkady's mind.

Whatever Ark was going through, we decided to stay together and stick with the status quo – live together and not bring anything up with our parents. But still I wanted real love, I wanted something deeper, I wanted a commitment so that I could be free about my relationship. In D.C. I became consumed by this feeling of not being able to love unconditionally without any judgment from my family. I wanted to have sex without guilt. I wanted to be me without any boundaries.

And along with my personal relationship being rocky, my job at the Social Security Administration wasn't going well either, mainly because I was bored and unchallenged. My workload, to put it mildly, was easy. Building statistical and economic models was second nature to me by now. For some people I guess easy work is good enough. But I didn't feel comfortable or fulfilled with easy. I'm perhaps a masochist of some sort because I thrive on at least a little stress and work pressure – and I often found myself looking at the clock and sensing that time was passing too slow, making me get sluggish energetically. The work just didn't stimulate me intellectually and so my usual spark of motivation was lagging.

My work as an analyst involved building models and writing reports for Congress. The Bush administration was pushing for privatization of Social Security and my job was to use census data and work with economists and actuaries to look ahead and project the impact of launching a new privatized SSA program on the population. We ran numbers, built out models and looked to see what those models would tell us.

The senior political appointee at SSA valued my ability to put together models and formal presentations that he could present to Congress. We discovered that we were both from Lawrence – he'd somehow made it to D.C. as a political appointee. He wanted me to work directly with him and I was afraid that this would cause some conflict with my direct boss. I just did my work – but like I said, it was boring for the most part.

What kept me engaged were my colleagues, people like Rhonda who would make me laugh incessantly and bring me pork rind to chew on. Rhonda was an African American woman with loads of confidence and raw humor. She grew up memorizing the dictionary and obtaining all the right pedigrees but her laughter was all her own.

A colleague of mine, a white male intern, revealed to me one day how much he was making, assuming that I was paid well – and the figure was significantly more than what I was making. That fact confirmed for me that it was time to leave. I voiced this disparity to my boss but nothing could be done about it, given the pay structure and how I'd been hired. They gave me monthly awards to compensate for the disparity and to recognize me but that didn't mean much to me. So I started seeking other jobs.

Doing international work felt like my true calling at that time – I wanted to be off in Africa and Asia, and I applied for related jobs, particularly at the World Bank. I think I applied nearly a hundred times, reaching out to different departments and people. I kept on getting rejections but I refused to feel discouraged. I no longer feared failure. I already had an okay job – I was now looking for my ideal job.

The one thing at SSA that I really liked was feeling like I was surrounded by people who were similar to me, I never had to prove anything – and I was hesitant to leave that situation because it was so comfortable. But one day I emailed a fellow Princeton alum, Victoria, who was at the World Bank. Almost overnight I received an email from one of her colleagues asking me to come in for an interview.

I went over in the middle of a work day during my lunch break, hopping on the metro from L'Enfant Plaza to Farragut West. I met with a woman named Kate who was the person doing the hiring, and that was the quickest interview ever. It felt like five minutes, with no emotions from my interviewer or myself throughout the simple Q&A format.

I left the interview feeling disappointed with my performance and the obvious lack of connection. The interview had been even worse than my mock videotaped interview back at Princeton. I had just completely failed to communicate how much I wanted to be at the World Bank and how hard I was willing to work to deliver.

I found myself back in my SSA cubicle next to Rhonda who was like, "Girl, you back already? What happened?" I told her that the interview didn't go at all well, and it had wrapped up too soon. We returned to our work – and then my phone rang, breaking the silence. I listened intently to each and every word that was spoken. My stomach and heart had the same feeling that I'd felt back when I got my letter of acceptance from Princeton.

It was Kate, who had just interviewed me, calling to let me know that she'd like me to join her team. As exciting as this news was, I had to decide carefully how to respond, because the position she was offering was a consultancy without any benefits such as healthcare. And I would start out in a short-term position with no guarantee beyond that. I'd have to give up stability and benefits to have my dream job. Should I stick with a stable and comfortable position or leap into an exciting and challenging position with lots of downsides if it didn't work out? I told Kate I'd think the offer over and get back to her.

Arkady was very supportive, encouraging me to take the risk. He even said he'd support me if things didn't pan out. My dad was also excited when I shared the news – but he was scared that it wasn't adequately stable. For me I saw that my worst-case scenario if the job didn't work out would be to move back to Lawrence. It was a no-brainer – I took the job. I didn't care about what the pay was. I just wanted to do something exciting. I wanted to do something that I could connect with. I knew overall that it would be a good experience even if I might not have a job in two months.

I gave my two-weeks' notice in mid-September 2003 and left after exactly one year at SSA. When I told my direct boss at SSA that I was leaving, she understood why I had to move on. And then … I started at the World Bank, again feeling that old fear. Can I really deliver? I'd be surrounded by brilliant people and I didn't know yet whether I belonged in their lofty midst. I would have a lot to prove.

It turned out that my job involved a lot of research and writing. Along with me, another woman had been hired around the same time. She was from Harvard but originally from Angola. She looked like a genuine African Queen with her natural beauty and radiant confidence. How could I compete with someone like her?

Kate, who was my immediate supervisor, told me on my first day that I should feel like I'm in a fire drill every minute. I said, "Yes, no problem." I mostly remained quiet and just did my job. I certainly never felt bored and time passed by so quickly that without my noticing, I often worked 12+ hours. I literally worked day and night and every weekend non-stop.

I didn't even take time off to attend my friends' wedding – Yes, Naeem and Mehvesh finally got married. But all I did was work. During this time I was still living with Arkady who was also working hard all the time. Somehow neither of us minded the long hours. It's a very good feeling to have work that's both satisfying and challenging.

Near the end of my short-term contract it seemed clear that my contract would probably not be renewed. Then I came into my office one morning – and my colleague from Angola was gone, her desk cleaned out and emptied … and I was still there! I wasn't sure what had happened and was too afraid to ask. I just went on with my tasks as usual.

Later that day I happened to check my bank for some reason and saw a direct deposit that was slightly higher than my usual paycheck. I went over to my office manager and asked if a mistake had occurred on my paycheck. "No," she said, "there's no mistake. You got a pay increase." I was never informed of this and I never broached the topic.

There was something about Kate that scared the shit out of me, so I continued to operate as if there was a fire drill every day. The level of stress was really high but I didn't necessarily show it. And each evening when I came home to Arkady, we didn't talk about work much. Our relationship was not faring well, it was in fact falling apart. I wanted more, it still felt wrong living with him without being married – and I was having a harder time holding these feelings inside. We argued a lot – but despite the fights and lack of future plans, for some reason we'd gone ahead and merged our bank accounts.

Arkady never counted how much he spent or I spent. Everything we had was shared. What was his was mine and vice versa. Ark was the opposite of Harold in Amy Tan's *Joy Luck Club* where a balance sheet was kept between him and Lena for every tiny expenditure. I think that in Ark's mind this trustful shared-finances step was a quiet commitment … a secret bond between the two of us.

But this hidden form of commitment and love didn't align with my Vietnamese culture. I didn't want our love to be hidden in some closet for only me and him to know about – and at some point that year I felt I'd had enough of all this uncertainty. I decided to ask him to marry me. It wasn't very romantic but he said yes. We even drove up to Princeton to pick out an engagement ring at Hamilton Jewelers.

The stone was small but it was a really beautiful ring. However, to be honest, I never really felt like this was quite real because I had been the one who'd asked to get married. I felt like something was missing and as usual I didn't know what he was really thinking. But I suppressed the need for romanticism – it just wasn't meant for me. It was a privilege of some sort reserved for the rich and the movies.

Meanwhile my professional life was going great, I was loving my job though my boss Kate yelled at me on a regular basis – I once got yelled at just for putting a comma in the wrong place. And it was still hard for me to write perfectly. But I was able to turn out solid 100-page reports when needed, even if that meant nail-biting every word and sentence in the middle of the night and on holidays or weekends. With my personal life in confusion, I threw myself harder into my work.

My department manager was Victoria, the Princeton alum who'd arranged my interview with Kate. Many of us were somewhat in awe of her for no particular reason, perhaps because she was so confident and good at what she did. I personally venerated Victoria and aspired to become that strong, confident woman one day. But back then I couldn't imagine ever attaining such a lofty goal.

Somehow Victoria always managed to find just the right moment to share some advice with me. On one occasion I was part of a committee that was organizing events, and I was supposed to speak in front of a group. I was deathly afraid to do this – and so Victoria talked to me. She told me simply that at some point I must grasp the courage to step up to the plate and assume an assigned leadership role – and that the time for me was now.

As I took in her words I realized that yes, the time had come for me to break free from all the subtle designated female roles and restricted responsibilities defined by my culture, where I was expected to stay meek, reticent, and subservient. A woman who was feeling dominant and empowered was antithetical to my cultural being.

Now Victoria was overtly challenging me to change and to explore – to push through glass boundaries that had always surrounded me. Since that day I've made many mistakes in flexing this leadership muscle. But I've at least somewhat taken the leap to assume roles that were not necessarily defined for me. Instead, I defined them myself. And I credit my growth over the years to Victoria.

Chapter Sixteen

~~~~~~~~~~~~~~~~~~~~~~~~~~~

At some point, I was finally assigned my first mission to Africa. Kate staffed me on a trip with a gentleman named Dan, who'd graduated from Princeton too. And quite soon after receiving the assignment (which I'd been hungering for) off we jetted to Benin in West Africa. This was my first mission for the U.N. and I didn't know at all what to expect. I was excited to be traveling to Africa working alongside Dan who was mentoring me.

The Bank flew us in First Class and I was a fish out of water in the fancy cabin. I mentioned my uncertainties regarding this assignment to Dan. As usual he was thoughtful in his response. He asked me to think about why I had been staffed on this mission. Obviously Kate felt I was up to the challenge. But still I felt an impostor on that trip, I just didn't know how I had suddenly arrived in this lofty situation, to be honest.

In short I had a fantastic time in Benin, a hot and humid country with its southern border on the Atlantic coastline. Benin is mostly an agricultural country, its main export is cotton. Catholicism is its main religion, with Islam also quite strong. There's also the local tribal traditional called Vodun, or Voodoo. It all sounded intriguing. Having been a French colony until 1960, many natives speak French there, which was to my benefit since I could speak a bit of the language. The coastline is known as the Slave Coast because so many captured natives had been taken from there to
~~~~~~~~~~~~~~~~~~~~~~~~~~~

the Americas. For fifteen years before 1990, the country had been a Marxist-Leninist state. Then after a coup it had become the Republic of Benin.

As I'd hoped, I felt a strange deep feeling of belonging while I was in that part of the world. I could relax naturally and just be myself. Dan and I had a most wonderful time out exploring this radically-different culture and climate. We even ventured to the Venice of Africa, a lake village called Ganvie. We took a boat and zigzagged through the narrow waterways and stopped here and there to converse with the natives. The stench of the water and flurry of mosquitos surrounding the makeshift homes on stilts felt more like my homeland world than the picturesque old world of Venice.

On one instance while off exploring with our guide, Dan and I sat at an outdoor plastic table and ordered *poulette bicyclette* from a cart on the road. As Dan was eating, he commented on how odd it was that the natives seemed to eat all of the chicken, including the cartilage on the bones. As he was saying this, I had just completely chewed off every piece of meat and cartilage on a drumstick bone, just the way we would in my mom's kitchen or in a village in Vietnam. I burst out laughing and showed Dan my cleaned bone. He looked at me and started laughing too.

The trip to Africa had been intense, and on my way flying back to America I asked permission to take a day or two off in Paris. Our flight flew through Paris from Benin so my solitary stop-over was easily arranged – and I was able to spend several days and nights quietly decompressing and reflecting. As I mentioned before, sitting on a bench all alone and content in that city provides a special meditative experience for me, and I now was able to look deeply at my relationship with Arkady. How could two people love each other so much, and have gone through so much together – and yet still be held apart by invisible forces?

I got back to D.C. and at first everything remained the same. I think I was afraid to upset my overall situation. I wasn't afraid of failure in general with my life – but I admit, I was afraid to give up on my mate relationship. I knew in my heart that Arkady loved me, he just didn't know how to love me the way I wanted. And also, he was so focused on his career that we had very little time together during that period.

Ark wanted intensely to succeed, to finally break away from his modest immigrant background and be able to live well, and also to help his parents. His father was still a taxicab driver in Boston. Ark wanted to be able to improve his parents' lives the same way that I wanted to help my family. Like Ark, I also wanted to succeed not just for myself, but to help my parents and siblings – to give them a more comfortable life.

Ark simply didn't think that starting a family at this time was the right thing to do, because it would impede him from achieving his other goals. So really, where did I fit in? I was obviously someone he wanted to be with but he didn't like all my constant pressure to formalize our relationship with a big marriage ceremony. When I returned from Africa I tried to push him to set a date so that we could start the planning – but my request just provoked more bickering.

Then at some point Ark began entertaining the idea of leaving corporate financial work and trying something quite new. And when his childhood friend asked him to join in a new venture, Ark seriously contemplated the decision. It would mean his moving back to Boston, leaving me and his job and moving back in with his parents. It seemed like I wasn't a factor in his decision-making, but I gave him my full support to pursue his dream, whether or not I was a part of that dream. I said, "You know, if you need to go back to Boston, go. If you want to build something, you should definitely do it because you don't want to have any regrets later on. If it doesn't work out you can always go back to a nine-to-five job. At this point you don't have any children or anyone to support. You can just go ahead and do it."

And so … he did. I helped him pack, and then drove him up to Boston. We stopped in Princeton to pick up some of our favorite foods at Hoagie Haven. The world of Princeton seemed a very long time ago. And now Ark was moving out of our apartment, headed back to live with his parents in Brighton. But we kept our shared bank account.

I returned to D.C. and made my own move finally – into a smaller apartment in Arlington, VA. And guess what – soon after Ark moved back to Boston he suddenly decided to give in to my desire to get married. I was immensely relieved! I didn't know what had provoked his change of heart. He just said one weekend that we should get married – and so we started to plan a wedding.

We agreed that all of our savings would go into paying for the wedding. At this time, Ark barely had any income.

I flew up multiple times to organize the wedding, but I never met Ark's parents as their son's fiancé – and I'd find out later that he never did tell them. Arkady's parents didn't even really know that we were together. They knew that I had been his friend from back in college, but that was that. Well, I think at some point they suspected there was something more going on. When his ex-girlfriend went to his parents' house to get something, Ark's mom inquired about me, asking if Ark and I were together. I wasn't the woman they wanted Ark to be with. So I guess when he moved back in with them, he hadn't shared much about his personal life.

My parents meanwhile did meet Arkady as my fiancé, and they were happy that I was going to get married and stop living, as my mother would put it, in sin together. One weekend Ark and I drove to Cape Cod and booked a very nice wedding place at the Chatham Inn. I started booking vendors and purchasing a beautiful wedding dress. I sent out all the invitations to my side of the family. Everything was finally flowing beautifully.

Then on my next trip to Boston to finalize a bunch of details two weeks before the wedding, I was sitting in a parking lot outside the florist where I had a meeting to wrap up the flower arrangement. I was feeling so elated, eager, thankful for the easy flow of preparations for the wedding. But just as I was heading into the flower store, my phone rang.

It was Arkady and I said brightly, "Hi!" He said, "Hi." Then there was silence. And finally he said: "I just can't."

I knew instantly what that meant.

Tears came rolling down my cheeks. I hung up. I felt so deeply shocked. Humiliated. Sad. Heartbroken. I called Naeem immediately and told him the news. He was speechless. And right then I had to go in and face the florist. I wiped my tears away and walked into a big bright room full of the scent of happy weddings – and told them that my wedding had been canceled. Of course I still had to pay for everything.

Then I drove home and told my parents that the wedding was not going to happen, that Arkady had backed out. What a disaster all around. Many of our friends and family had already booked their trip to Boston. My uncle in California who had helped put me through college, who had come to the states with us – he had to be told. And all my friends from college and grad school had booked their tickets.

When I told my parents, I think their hearts sank right down into the ground. They thought that maybe I wasn't good enough for Arkady's family, and sadly they accepted this as part of life. And oh, the humiliation of their having to admit to everyone that I had been so rudely jilted!

So – what was I to do? I just wanted to get far away from home, so I headed back to D.C. feeling numb and depressed. I was supposed to be away for a few weeks to honeymoon in Bora Bora. Instead I was sitting totally alone in D.C. It was just terrible. Luckily my dear friend Ajai called me. He and I often spent time together, he worked at the World Bank too, and we often had lunch together and dinners when we were both working late. He knew everything that was going on in my life – and when I came back to D.C. he called me saying that I needed to get my ass out of D.C. now. Ajai never swears, unlike me, and he literally said he would kick my ass if I didn't get out of D.C. and take a break.

I caved and did what he suggested. I looked for cheap tickets somewhere, anywhere. Since I'd spent most of my savings on the wedding and couldn't get refunds, I searched for the most affordable flight to anywhere far away. I thought maybe Hawaii would do, but I hated the idea of Hawaii. When I was living in

California it seemed like everyone who had money went to Hawaii. It was so cliché. But I found a ticket for around $500 roundtrip, and decided what the hell, I'll go.

So I flew over and fell in love with the aloha state of mind. It seemed like most people there were similar to me, everyone was either Asian or half Asian or something. And everyone was so nice and friendly. My favorite foods were there – Spam and rice was okay to order without being judged. The weather and local culture somehow brought me back into some faint memories of my early childhood – hot and humid, Asian people, Spam and rice.

I rented a car and drove around the entire island of Oahu. I sat on beaches by myself with no one in sight, beautiful deserted beaches. I went for day hikes, and rode a bike with a group for a day. This was the second time in my life on a bike, I was afraid because I didn't have any confidence in my biking skills. But I decided to do a bike tour and I actually survived and loved it!

I basically did what I used to do when I was in Paris, which means I explored Hawaii in solitude. I also met up with the parents of my old Bowdoin flame Chris. His mom quite generously took me all around her neighborhood. We went for Jamba Juice and walked along the beach – and she gave me some words of wisdom that I took to heart, about how everything, including my canceled wedding, happens for a reason.

Most people don't have words to share, they don't know what to say to someone who's had their heart broken like I had. But she was there for me and that was so wonderful. I truly loved Hawaii for giving me a place to reflect and to heal. Hawaii was special the same way that California, Paris and Seattle were special.

Chapter Seventeen

Somehow when I returned to D.C. I went back to work immediately. I just plunged back into work, drank a lot of wine in my off time … and somehow got by. But I couldn't just shut Arkady out of my heart. Our relationship was certainly a strange one, but it ran deep. He didn't call me on the phone and try to explain his decision – but I knew that the driving factor in his abrupt cancellation of the wedding had been because he loved his parents and ultimately, even though he wanted to make me happy, he just couldn't bring himself to hurt them.

Then one night, about a month after the wedding cancellation, he suddenly appeared at my door in D.C. He'd told everyone back in Boston that he was going off somewhere on a trip, but not to D.C. He'd come down just to see me – and of course I took him in. He was obviously caught in a terrible internal struggle even though he couldn't verbalize it. His heart told him to be with me but his mind said no. So … yes, I'd been deeply hurt, but I didn't reject him.

He came to visit me quite often, like he had before, as if the wedding thing hadn't ever happened at all. Then he'd go back up to his parents in Boston. At first it was a lonely time for me, living in solitude after two full years in D.C. living with Ark. But then I started to go out a little in the evenings and on weekends. I'd casually meet up with people I knew from work, or some other acquaintances, and step by step I quite effortlessly began to build a group of new friends like Debby, Tara, Aida, and Jane. And I started to spend more time with old friends like Ajai, Rodney, Has and Reggie.

I found myself doing various things that I hadn't done back when I was living with Arkady. I began a new life, exploring different restaurants and coffee shops and spending hours in museums and just taking quiet walks here and there. Now that I think about it, I actually had a very satisfying time in D.C. after Arkady left. I didn't want to be home alone so I went out and met new people who helped to enrich my life.

It was good times – but I also have to admit that I would still break down in tears at random periods of the day. I went to the dentist a few months after the wedding cancellation and right there in the dentist chair I started crying. The dentist didn't know what to do and so he just sat me up to let me cry it out.

But in general during the day I was fine. At nights and weekends I was okay if I went out to indulge in good friends and wine and lots of jazz. Also I still loved my job. Being at the Bank was a dream job because I felt fully accepted, and I was continually growing.

My fears of handling the workload had mostly dissipated after my African trip to Benin. And there was so much diversity in my office – my team included people from Côte d'Ivoire, Ethiopia, India, Europe, Asia. We became a very tight-knit group. We were like family. Whenever one of us had an issue or problem, even personal, we would all meet up and talk it through. And meanwhile we worked so hard together. I felt accepted. I felt finally free to just be myself.

The overall Bank atmosphere reminded me of when I'd been over in Southeast Asia – I just felt like I naturally belonged. I loved how the diversity of thinking and culture allowed room for people like me. Everyone was obviously from their own unique background and we all honored and embraced each other's differences. This was what I'd wanted for so long.

I admit that at first I'd felt a little terrified because I wasn't sure I'd be able to deliver or meet expectations, especially with all the written reports that were required. But I worked very long and hard hours and finally started to feel confident that I could handle my assignments. The only stress came with making sure we had the right analysis and fully trustworthy data, because these papers got published.

My old feelings of insecurity, of being an imposter, at least temporarily went away during that phase of my life. But I always credited my success to all my hard work – I never let myself believe that it was my innate intelligence. When someone would say to me, "Oh, you're so smart," I'd say something like, "Yeah, street smart, throw me in the hood and I'll figure it out." Mehvesh to this day hates it when I talk this way. But that's how I honestly felt – and I put all my self-esteem into being a hard worker, and I guess there's nothing wrong with that.

So yes, at the early age of 25 I felt comfortable working at the Bank, I enjoyed it more and more – and I especially loved my assignments traveling to places like Rwanda, Kenya and Uganda. I traveled with my boss and also another person who became my mentor. And then I was staffed on an assignment to travel to the

Middle East and North Africa – to Tunisia, then Jordan, then Yemen.

I loved even the difficult and dangerous situations that arose during that trip. Just before arriving in Jordan, for instance, our hotel there had exploded. I could have canceled because of the obvious dangers, but those things somehow didn't scare me. Regardless of the tough current situations, I just loved being in those countries, absorbing their local cultures, their abject challenges and brave hopes and everything – I seemed to thrive when I was over there, almost to blossom inside with new feelings. Even now, whenever I go back to that region of the world I'm in heaven.

During that time my work took me thankfully away from my personal problems. But when I came home I ended up drinking quite a bit. Whenever I was alone in my apartment I found myself turning on some jazz and kicking back with a few glasses of red wine. I barely ate, and this was of course quite unhealthy. I was really tiny for my height, I was about 5'6" and 105 lbs. I'd lost weight from the parasites on that first trip to Africa, and my unhealthy lifestyle had kept the weight off.

So yeah, I barely slept, all I did was work or hang out and drink and listen to jazz – I guess it could be said that I was drowning in my relationship sorrow. And then Arkady would show up. I couldn't turn him away. I knew that in his heart he wanted to be with me. So I took him back each time he showed up at my doorstep.

We started seeing each other again, still mostly secretive as far as our parents and Boston friends were concerned. It was awkward all around, but it went on for months. And then – Ark said to me a second time, "Let's get married." So when I came up to Boston the next time, we went out looking for a venue. We found a mansion in Back Bay that hosted weddings. Most of our savings had been spent on our previous attempt at a wedding but we said to each other, "Okay, we can do this. We can save and we can make the wedding smaller." To secure the date, all we had to do was return to Back Bay with a deposit. Arkady said that he'd take care of it.

I left Boston for D.C. and right away was scheduled to travel to East Africa. I temporarily forgot wedding plans and all that because really, I fell in love with Africa all over again on that trip. It seemed like I was falling in love with so many places. East Africa seemed just so in sync with my own deeper inner realms. But then the excursion was over and I had to go get on a plane in Nairobi and fly back home. And while still on the lane taxiing to the gate, I turned my phone on and checked my messages.

My eyes began to water, my heart dropped to the floor and sharp pains hit me in my chest and overwhelmed me as I listened to a week-old voicemail from the woman at the Back Bay mansion. She was saying that Arkady had never shown up with the deposit. Tears flowed hot down my cheeks. I knew exactly what that message meant.

Everything was a blur, a terribly disorienting déjà vu experience, my very own Groundhog Day. I went straight to my apartment. I don't remember if I called Arkady. I don't know what I did. I just carried on as best I could for some undefined period of time. And then … Arkady showed up at my door again. He wanted to be forgiven, to be together with me – but I exploded at him with biting accusations. Why was he doing this to me? Did he need me just for sex? Why was he jerking me around like a stupid puppet? What about my feelings! Did they matter to him at all? If he truly loved me, why was he putting me through all this agonizing pain over and over again – couldn't he see how much I was suffering inside?

He had no response, he never showed any emotions around all our struggles, or talked with me about what was going on between us. After six years together we knew each other so intimately on certain fronts, but on others we were, as they say, worlds apart. Our family and cultural backgrounds were so opposite from each other – Russian versus Vietnamese, Jewish versus Buddhist-Catholic. We were both from immigrant families but we came from opposite ends of the Earth.

But what were we to do? We were entangled seemingly hopelessly with each other at heart levels but I never really knew what he was feeling about things like family and marriage. He simply couldn't talk about why he kept on doing what he did to me. He would fly down once or twice a month and be mostly considerate and loving to me – and then abruptly leave me when the weekend was over because he had to get back to work.

He was still doing the startup and I was helping him pay some of the bills. He barely made anything so I was supporting him as best I could. I believed in his startup, in his budding entrepreneurial spirit. And really, the reason I took him back in was because I knew that in his heart he wanted us to stay together. He was blindly struggling with something and I couldn't just walk away. Sure, I also was in pain – but I felt it was easier for me to be hurt than for me to hurt him.

If Ark had just walked away and never come back, I would have moved on. I would have been okay. But our bond was so much deeper than just good sex. I knew it wasn't about sex because it would have been much easier for him to hook up with someone in Boston – but he never did. His friends tried to arrange for him to be with a gorgeous blond Russian woman – but that person would tell me years later that she could see in Arkady's eyes that he was still in love with me.

At one point he said to me, "Let's just elope, let's go to Hawaii where you had such a wonderful time." So I booked tickets for Hawaii – and of course just before that trip he called me and said he couldn't come because his grandmother was sick. So … I lost money then too. I'd been stood up for a third time.

But he promised fervently that he wouldn't do that ever again – and he asked me to come up and look for a new venue. I flew up and we went out together and found a place in Boston known as the Omni Parker House. We went to tour it, put a deposit down, and then came back on another occasion for the tasting and menu selection. I sent out invitations and an email explaining how to get around Boston.

And … that was canceled too. Enough Groundhog Day! That fourth time was it for me. I remember sending an email to everyone saying that this wedding has been canceled indefinitely. I would have no bachelorette party, no bridal shower, nothing. I suppose all this marriage drama would seem comical from a distance. But looking back, I think my friends thought I was crazy. They just couldn't grasp why I was subjecting myself to this over and over again. And it's true, I would never want my daughter or my sons to go through what I went through. No way would I want them to be with someone who did what Arkady did.

But my parents were thankfully okay, they felt for me. They accepted my struggle with Arkady, even if it took many attempts to finalize our relationship. That's just how things go, they would say, life is not so easy, especially in America. They were never upset with me. They just felt my pain. My uncle in California called my dad, talking about how I was someone who just always struggled in life, how nothing ever came easy to me.

I went back to D.C., bit back my tears – and then went off on another Bank trip to the Middle East. I'd definitely had enough of Arkady. After four cancelations, all the money was gone. It was time to put that man behind me. I was now 27 and this was the time to move on. This was what I was saying to myself like a mantra as my plane took off – move on! Without Ark in my life things would be so clear and simple and fulfilling. What was this demon of romantic love anyway? Who needed it. I was solidly on my much-desired path to success, and who knows, down the road I'd probably find my Cary Grant to make my life really complete.

Chapter Eighteen

~~~~~~~~~~~~~~~~~~~~~~~~~~~~~~

I admit I probably over-romanticized about the Middle East and North Africa, but it really felt like the Arabian Nights whenever I was over there. I was assigned to work on gender and development in the Middle East, and one week I flew over and attended an all-women conference in Tunisia. I could communicate fairly well there because I spoke French – and I met so many wonderful Arabs. I was doing my best to understand their side of the complex Israeli-Palestinian conflict, and especially trying to understand all the related women's issues.

Most of the women at the conference seemed quite strong, confident, and beautiful. There were so many divergent viewpoints on women's rights – some of the conference participants wanted to blatantly push the limits of their culture, while others were still willing to pursue these rights within their traditional religious and cultural norms.

At this conference in Tunisia I also met two gentlemen, both from Egypt and both with the same first name, Omer. We had a good time getting to know one another. It was a multi-day conference and after the conference each evening we would explore Tunis – all those white buildings with Mediterranean-blue doors lining the coast.

Tunisia was so beautiful, like Greece with the winter sun shining bright and kissing my face. It was just gorgeous. We walked along
~~~~~~~~~~~~~~~~~~~~~~~~~~~~~~

roads lined with small shops as we chatted and laughed and shared all the sensory delights. They were such gentlemen, always holding the door for me and letting me go first or drink or eat first. I felt special and that felt good.

I meanwhile kept in touch with my family back home, and I did briefly chat with Arkady. I didn't tell him I'd decided to leave him, that wasn't something to do over the phone. I just told him I was doing well and enjoying my adventure in foreign lands. This was in 2005 and Arkady and my family were naturally a little concerned that I was traveling through the war-torn Middle East, but I felt safe enough.

After Tunisia, my boss and I went on to Jordan, which I also found to be just lovely. I experimented with food in Jordan, including lamb tartar. I'd never eaten raw meat like that before, but it was actually pretty good. Overall I found the food in the whole region to be absolutely mouthwatering.

The men struck me as gorgeous. And also in the Middle East everyone was just so nice, so welcoming to us – and also quite completely different from what the news back home portrayed them to be.

I soon found that in the Middle East, people I met did not like to know that I was an American. There was deep tension on that point. When someone asked me where I was from and I said, "America," they'd say, "No, where are you originally from?" When I said I was from Vietnam, they would rejoice and talk about how my people had defeated the whole U.S. military. My guide who took me around after my meetings put me on a pedestal because I was Vietnamese and Vietnam was the only country that had beaten the U.S. in a war.

And then we took off for Yemen. Being in that culture felt like arriving in the medieval ages. I was staying in Sana'a, an ancient city surrounded by vast deserts and bleak mountains. The country was obviously extremely poor. The men wore daggers on their hips, mostly made of hardwood. And they were chewing *qat*, a leaf that's a stimulant and gave them a slight high. The wad in their mouth made them look like they had a golf ball in their cheeks.

Yemen was such a different world from Jordan and Tunisia, very traditional and religious. All the women were completely covered from head to toe, and I had to sit in a separate room from the men when I ate, and also cover my head. The one time I didn't cover my head with a scarf, suddenly there were angry men chasing me and yelling at me. I had to quickly cover up – then they calmed down and walked away.

When I was in mixed company it was so strange that all I could see of the women were their eyes – they were quite intense! And then the moment I was in a meeting with them with no men present they would take their burqas off. I was somehow surprised to see that they had makeup on, and were wearing beautiful outfits – so sexy to see what was hidden underneath their drab black burqas.

I also found out that even in Yemen there were lingerie stores and wedding dresses and all these feminine things – but they couldn't display them to anyone except in a room of only women, or of course with their husbands. Still they were strong women, confident and hungry for change. Spending time in Yemen was a very meaningful and powerful experience for me.

Well, then it was time to head back to Dulles. I parted ways with my boss after we deplaned, and walked through the terminals and exited customs, headed toward the taxi stand – and there was Arkady, waiting for me. I don't think I'd even told him my flight number or the time of arrival, I just told him that I was coming back on the afternoon of this particular day.

We stood there and hugged – and believe it or not, he right away asked me if I wanted to go get married immediately, tomorrow. My reaction to this offer? I didn't feel any sense of joy or excitement. Without any reflecting I found myself saying yes – but I didn't feel anything. I didn't feel anything like a blushing bride in love. The pain of the recent past was very much still there, along with the lingering love.

The next day came around and we went off to the courthouse down the street from where I was living. We got married. It was a chilly December day in 2005. It was, to say the least, anticlimactic. And I admit that after the short bland civil ceremony I didn't feel like we were really married. It didn't feel real. We'd used a ring from the first planned-and-derailed wedding. And sadly, during that entire day I was wondering if I'd just made a terrible mistake. Part of me actually didn't seem to want him anymore. And then time was up and he went off. Alone. Back to Boston.

Also I'd find out later that he didn't tell his parents he was married. They found out by chance because two months later, when I sent him a Valentine's Day card, they happened to read it – and on the card it said in my handwriting, "Happy Valentine's Day To My husband." I later heard that his dad, Yakov, was so upset that he screamed, "What the fuck is this!"

And on my side, the elopement didn't soothe any of my feelings about my relationship and future with Arkady. It actually seemed to make things worse. I eventually told my parents but they refused to accept this civil approach to marriage. How could they tell their friends and family that we had gotten married without inviting the family – and without a formal ceremony of some sort?

For Arkady's parents and family, the whole situation was painful for a number of reasons. I mentioned earlier that they hadn't been invited to attend his brother's wedding, which they'd also disapproved of. Arkady's family lived a very modest life, they had worked very hard for their sons and they naturally wanted what they thought would be best for their future.

Unfortunately for me and Ark, this meant his marrying a Russian Jewish wife and preserving their cultural and religious heritage. Coming from the former Soviet Union where they hadn't even been allowed to practice their religion, they now wanted to rebuild an extended family that openly celebrated their culture and religion. They wanted to finally relax in the new country and fully enjoy a happy Jewish Russian family life with their sons and grandchildren.

So yes, I could understand why Ark had been secretive about our marriage. He had to deal with an impossible internal struggle – to hurt his parents or hurt the person he loved. He also must have thought about his career and whether he could support a family with his new and risky business venture. And anyway, when his parents found out that we had eloped, like my own parents they didn't believe in the civil certificate. They simply didn't accept the marriage.

It soon became clear to me that none of our parents could live with things as they were – the piece of paper from some judge down in Virginia didn't mean anything to them. And in fact, nor did it to me. I didn't feel any sort of wedding bliss or honeymoon joy. And even though I wore my ring, since I was technically married, I didn't feel married in my heart, I didn't even know if I still wanted to be with Arkady – so what, should we annul the marriage?

Meanwhile nothing had really changed, we still got together every few weeks, we had enjoyable sex and we carried on with our friendship. But that was it. This was a very dark time for me. All that saved me was my work. That was to be my future. I would continue and succeed in the World Bank, I would have my career, my independence, my lifeline to feeling valued and content .

It was during these difficult months after our civil marriage that my doctor informed me that I was infertile and would never be able to have any children. The medical report stated: "This patient presents with menometrorrhagia and infertility." That was such a shock. I hadn't really thought about being a mother, that wasn't at all on my agenda.

I'd of course always been careful about pregnancy because my father had been so worried that I'd get knocked up in high school or college and ruin my professional career. But finding out that I'd never have children – this somehow both relieved me, confused me, and upset me. Well, at least I could finally stop worrying about getting pregnant.

One evening later on that spring I was at my office working really late. A friend, colleague, and fellow Princeton alum, Shonar, was also working late. We were the only ones left in our unit. As I was walking out, I greeted her good night. She looked up at me curiously and asked, "Hey, how are you doing, Mai? What's up with you, are you pregnant?" I of course retorted, "No of course not, what are you talking about?" And she said right back, "Seriously, you look pregnant." What was she talking about? "Are you saying that I look fat? Do I have a tummy?" I asked. "Well, there's just something about your face," she said.

I knew I couldn't be pregnant, but I rushed over to CVS to get a pregnancy test, came back to the World Bank bathroom, did the ttest, waited.

Oh, my gosh – I'm pregnant.

This especially jolted me because a few weeks before, Arkady had come down to visit and we'd gone to PF Chang's over in Virginia for dinner. They'd brought us fortune cookies and mine had said that I would be hearing a child's laughter soon. We thought the fortune message was purely random and rather odd – but not related to us at all. I'd just put aside the whole incident as meaningless.

Most of my personal associations with childbirth and motherhood had come from my own radical beginnings. I'd heard so many times how difficult a baby I'd been, crying all the time, and how my parents had struggled immensely to keep me alive while we made our escape to America. As a result, I guess I'd always seen children as a burden to be avoided. And on top of that, getting pregnant was generally considered to be the beginning of the unfortunate death of a woman's career goals – and my work was the main thing that was keeping me afloat in life.

Arkady was in Boston when I got that positive test result. I went home totally shaken, trying to figure out the best way to tell him.

Finally I just called him up without any plan and vomited it out: "I'm pregnant." Silence on the other end. I remember asking him what was he feeling, and he said, "Nothing." It didn't hit him at all. And there was certainly zero joy or jubilation.

So there we were, a young couple technically married and now with child – but with none of our parents accepting our marriage as valid. I knew my parents would be totally embarrassed to have a daughter with child out of wedlock. So I decided that we would need to right away stage a formal family wedding.

But I could easily imagine, even after we formalized our union, that people would assume Arkady got married because he'd knocked me up – or worse still, that I had purposely gotten pregnant in order to push him into marriage. Very few people knew that we had already eloped months before. Rumors would fly and our parents would feel devastated.

I had no idea what Arkady was feeling or thinking. I didn't even know what I myself was feeling or thinking. Our circumstances were definitely not conducive to bringing a child into the world. Emotionally our union felt like a sham, physically we were in a long-distance relationship, and financially Ark was still working with little pay toward perhaps building something viable. We just weren't ready for parenthood.

But I went to my doctor again and it was true – I was definitely pregnant and the baby would soon get bigger and bigger inside me. I called up my parents and told them. They displayed no emotions over the phone but they informed me that I must immediately have a wedding, and in their minds a wedding consisted of a couple saying their vows in a religious ceremony with a priest, all in front of family and the community.

That was the extent of their reaction. But when Arkady told his parents, his father's reaction was much more explosive and his verbal declaration especially painful: "I don't want yellow grandchildren."

But Ark and I never discussed not keeping the baby. We both simply assumed that the baby was going to expand us into a family of three. We needed a wedding celebration of some sort as soon as possible. I flew up to Boston and we called around to see who had an opening. The Fairmont had a date on June 10th. We secured it and had a month to plan everything. We had to go through our list and start cutting. We gave our parents and their friends and family priority, as this wedding was mostly for them. So, here we go again, I thought. Fifth time's the charm?

Ark's family required a Jewish religious ceremony so we set that up. I quickly made invitations by hand, and sent them out. I had the wedding dress from the first time around and it was starting to get tight. I went back down to D.C. and to work. I remember being in a daze. Things were happening to me, I wasn't in charge. I couldn't see into my own future at all. I just had to get beyond the marriage ceremony.

When I came back to Boston for the wedding I remember my main emotion was being nervous that Arkady was again not going to show up. I had my hair done and I did my own makeup. The Gay Pride Parade was happening that weekend in Boston and streets were closed, and it was raining. We had the same rabbi we'd canceled several times before. When I got to the Fairmont I saw Arkady dressed in his suit. He'd showed up. My nerves instantly disappeared.

Then something truly heartening happened. Arkady's father and my father sat down together on a couch, meeting each other for the very first time. While final preparations were made, the two fathers watched the World Cup together, Argentina versus the Ivory Coast. Both dads could barely communicate with each other but they were both cheering for Argentina, and they seemed to just let go and bond right then and there – and somehow everything suddenly lightened up.

After the ceremony was finished my dad for the first time in a long time stroked my head as his way of saying I love you. He had a big smile. Like I said before, my parents didn't care how many times it took to get to this point. They only cared that it was finally happening. And for me also, it didn't matter that four other wedding attempts had failed. The fifth happened.

And I saw later in photographs that Ark's father was also feeling proud. He shared with my father the unspoken bond of two immigrants who were still struggling in America, but whose children seemed to be doing well. Both felt very pleased that we were able to hold a wedding at a fancy place. Ark hadn't ever talked much about it, but his dad had had a really tough life. He'd been raised by his two big sisters in Russia while his mom worked a menial job. They were so poor they barely had food. Ark's dad never had a father figure and he struggled terribly through childhood.

I was able step by step to let go of resentment toward Arkady's parents, because I knew they'd struggled so much to give their all to their boys. Arkady had been eleven when Gorbachev opened the doors to allow Jews to leave for the U.S. or Israel or whatever country would accept them. When Arkady arrived in America he only had one pair of pants. He wore them every day to school and people made fun of him – but he had learned the hard way back in Russia not to let anything upset him. He just did his best to study because education was seen as the door to a better future, which in fact it was.

Only after our marriage did I come to understand Ark better. Like everyone, he was the result of his childhood, his culture, his religion, his family heritage. He and I were so different in so many ways, but we obviously shared deep immigrant bonds which underpinned everything we did together.

We all celebrated that evening together. I have pictures of everyone joyfully dancing and drinking. When the traditional Jewish dance music came on and everyone was going around in circles, the event felt priceless. Like it or not, we were married, we were going to have a baby – and we would just have to somehow adjust. I returned solo back to my apartment and my work at the World Bank, and at first I simply couldn't imagine giving up my job. I thought we could just continue living separately and I'd carry on somehow down in D.C. I wasn't going to let my matrimonial fate destroy my entire life.

But then one weekend Ark came down and tried to talk sense into me. He said I simply had to move back up to Boston where we had family to help us. We were acting like two stunned creatures, we hadn't even considered parenthood – so this was such foreign territory. We still argued and banged heads, but we were both conscious of the new life growing inside me.

After Ark left I finally started to think at least somewhat realistically. Of course he was right – I wouldn't be able to raise the baby by myself in D.C. while I also kept working. My parents all lived in the Boston area. It would be best to raise our child with grandparents around. I'd worked my whole life to secure a job which I loved, where I was respected, where I had a future. But I finally saw that I had no choice. It obviously wasn't the fault of my unborn child that I gave my six-months' notice to Victoria and Kate. Like my parents had done with me back in Vietnam, love brings people together and that flow naturally brings about whatever fate has in store for us.

During those final six months I just worked and worked, trying to wrap things up. But a curious thing started happening. It became harder for me to get work done – not because I was pregnant but because I began to feel bored with my work, the same feeling I'd had when I was working at the Social Security office. There was somehow no more challenge. I started taking things slower and slower, like I was dragging my feet.

I got really big. I gained sixty pounds because I used the pregnancy as a license to eat everything, especially chocolate cupcakes. At some point I could hardly walk, my hips got dislocated and I was miserable. It was tough, I was barely holding on. So Arkady decided to come down and stay in D.C. for the remainder of my work and pregnancy. He drove me to work every day and picked me up. He was very kind, and I needed that kindness very much right then.

I was due in early December. Thanksgiving holidays rolled around and it was just me and Arkady. After Thanksgiving my mom came down – just in time for me to give birth in early December. My mom was in the delivery room with me and Arkady. Around six o'clock I was ready to push. I don't remember but my mom said I cursed like crazy even though she believed a woman should deliver in silence. I had no idea birthing could be so agonizingly painful. But finally my baby came all the way out and they almost immediately put her in my arms.

I was in a terrible state of mind, and it developed into a strong case of post-partem blues. I would cry at random times, I was just entirely overwhelmed, I couldn't cope. All I can do in retrospect is ask for forgiveness – and maybe perhaps forgive myself too – for not being a very good mother back then.

Meanwhile my daughter, Leah, had her own sometimes life-threatening difficulties. She was a colicky baby like I had been before her. My pediatrician thought she was getting too much milk and told me not to feed her more than X amount of milk. So I fed her exactly what the doctor said – but as it turned out, she was actually needing more milk. So just like I'd nearly starved as a baby because my mother wasn't eating enough to make milk for me, my own baby was half-starving because of the doctor's orders. Very strange.

Also Leah's jaundice was quite severe, often above the extreme level. We had to rush her into the hospital where she was put in the incubator naked because they were trying to get her bilirubin levels down. That treatment worked temporarily, but as soon as we came home her symptoms would return. I'd call the doctor and she wouldn't believe me. I'd plead with her, please, something's still wrong. We'd take her in again and they'd prick her finger – and yes, her bilirubin levels were over the extreme limits again.

That happened three times. They couldn't figure out what was going on so we then went to Georgetown University's Medical Center to see a specialist. They discovered she had something called G6PD Deficiency which is a rare enzyme deficiency that blocks her absorption of breast milk. So I had to stop giving her breast milk and give her formula instead.

This all happened while we were still in D.C., I'd only taken two weeks off for maternity leave and had to return to work to wrap up before leaving at the end of January – but I couldn't stop crying. Those first two months were agonizing, I barely slept. I was a mess mentally, physically, everything. Then the end of January came around and my brother and his wife came down to help us pack everything.

And so Ark, myself and Leah moved into my parents' house in Lawrence, in fact into my old bedroom. We lived there for eight months because we didn't have money to rent our own place. My parents were over the moon having a grandchild in the house. But Arkady's parents at first were very distant emotionally, and they were both still working. They didn't embrace our new family the way we expected.

I had no job. It was full-time work taking care of Leah. And it was difficult living again with my parents after being gone so long – just a little over ten years since I went off to college. My parents expected me to live by their rules and act like I was fifteen, even though I was now a responsible adult and a mom. So we had a lot of tension. Did I really sign up for this?

Once I settled in, I started looking for work. There seemed to be zero international-development jobs in Boston. Well, I did connect with someone through a friend. But when she learned that I had an infant she wrote me an email, saying bluntly that she didn't think I would be effective in my role, with a child and all.

That really stung – not because I was rejected but because I wasn't even given a chance.

I somehow found another lead, an organization that really liked me and brought me in for an interview. I'd worked earlier in D.C. on a project similar to what they were doing. The only problem was that they couldn't match my World Bank salary. I'd have to accept a $25,000 pay cut but we really needed the income – so I took it.

Arkady and I really wanted to move out of my parents' house as soon as possible. We started saving and soon we had enough to put a down-payment on a two-bedroom apartment. For my work I had to commute to Cambridge which took me two hours but at work I was fine with my assignments and able to deliver quickly. The problem was that I delivered so fast that they started increasing my workload.

Arkady was often traveling for his startup, which was focused on financial training. He was gone teaching at different places – and that left me alone with Leah. I had to find super-efficient ways to care for her. When I got home around dark we had some time together while I also cooked and took care of the house. Then the minute I put her to bed I did office work until three o'clock or so, slept a few hours – then woke up, fed and dressed Leah, dropped her off at a Russian daycare and headed to work – then I'd come back, pick her up, feed her, take her to the park, come back to the apartment and read to her, put her to bed … and start working again.

I would also almost compulsively clean the entire house – I think that cleaning became my way of feeling in control of my life. And I was still feeling depressed but I tried not to show it, tried not to cry in public. I also very soon came to hate my job. They took advantage of my workaholic nature and constantly overloaded me without paying me fairly for my actual hours.

More and more I was feeling like I just couldn't handle the stress of raising Leah alone. Working eighty hours a week, I'd become very mechanical with Leah and that wasn't fair to her. So after eight months, Ark and I found time to talk together and think our situation through. His company was doing better now, our situation was thankfully improving on that front. And after he heard me out, Ark supported my decision to quit my job.

I felt greatly relieved. I'd hated feeling guilty about not having more time to focus on my daughter. She'd had such a rocky beginning on so many fronts. I wanted change, I wanted somehow to shift into a more normal life where I could take time to appreciate how bright and witty and fun my daughter was!

Then the financial crisis started hitting us along with the rest of the country. Arkady had built his finance-training company to include a number of employees and he was concerned about not wanting to lay off anyone. As I was unemployed at the time, I started looking for ways to help him with the business. I'd never done that sort of analysis before but his office manager had recently left, and I fairly quickly identified several new ways to steer the ship.

So I took the leap and started working for Ark and his partner. They liked what I was doing and soon things were really running well. Also I was able to do my work very quickly and this left me with plenty of time to take care of Leah and be with her more. I also found that the entrepreneurial world was really quite fun, very different from research, economics and analysis. I was now doing operational work, and I found other areas in the company where they needed improvements and I could be of help.

I became pregnant again but I continued helping Arkady and his partner. In the end they never had to let anyone go, they were successfully weathering the storm. This was in 2009. I grew bigger with my second child but I didn't get really fat. It was so different than the first pregnancy – I was in a better place emotionally. And when it was time to deliver, my mom was there again but the delivery was really fast.

My state of mind was so different this time around. With Leah I'd had no idea what to expect, I'd felt entirely unready for motherhood. This second time around, when they put my son in my arms I was able to be present, to tap into the natural human process of birthing. I wanted to hold him the whole night. I was finally feeling those birthing instincts active inside me.

Also, everything following birth went vastly better because my son didn't suffer from colic, he didn't cry hardly at all. He was such a happy baby that I thought, hey, I can have many more babies. I had almost no post-partem blues this time.

PART SEVEN

~~~~~~~~~~~~~~~

Boston/Vietnam
~~~~~~~~~~~~~~~

Chapter Nineteen

During this second post-birthing period I continued working a lot with Arkady, and I also joined the board of several nonprofits and then sat on Boston's election advisory committee. I was still admittedly a workaholic, even though I no longer needed to be. Ever since my own birth and early childhood, non-stop work and struggle had been the model of my parents – and I guess I just inherited the compulsion to always be busy.

I remember that I even kept working during my son's delivery, sending off some emails from my hospital bed. I just liked being busy, being in motion in my body and my mind – feeling that I was constantly in control of my schedule and my life. And yes, as therapists would explain to me, in retrospect I can see that I used my continual focus on work and external problems to help me avoid some deeper issues that were continuing unresolved inside me.

With this in mind, I can now see that during the next year or so, with two children to take care of and also keeping myself a slave to my chronic work schedule, my mental condition started to deteriorate again. Ark was still almost never around, he was as usual fully consumed in his teaching/training work, constantly traveling and absent from our home.

From a broader perspective, ever since I'd found out I was pregnant the first time down in D.C. I'd been locked in manic gear. This had gone on for over three years now, and it seems that ultimately I couldn't carry on that way forever without breaking down. And as I continued with non-stop mothering and work and volunteer responsibilities, I was starting to feel that my whole life was pressing in on me, I felt more and more dull and miserable.

I didn't actually realize this consciously, but both my mood and my energy began to drop down. I had usually been full of can-do energy, springing up in the mornings and plunging into the work at hand. But now that zest for life had begun to ebb more and more, finally reaching the point where I could hardly get myself up and out of bed in the mornings.

This had never happened before. I wasn't physically sick, I was just mentally and emotionally slipping under the weather. But as my depression progressed I failed to heed the warning signs. Instead I struggled to stay bright and positive, to be a good mother and also constantly 'out there' helping others – but not helping myself.

I survived like this for a while longer, but ultimately I wasn't able to fight off my downward-plunging moods, I just couldn't make the demons go away. They would sneak up and overtake me when I least expected them. More and more, my heart felt so heavy that everything seemed hopeless, finally reaching the point where I got zero joy out of being present. I felt like something had been chasing after me all my life – and now it had finally caught up and grabbed me.

I finally broke down and told my doctor about all my various symptoms, and he immediately wanted me to visit a therapist. I hardly believed in therapy, I'd been brought up believing that we all had to take care of our own internal problems on our own, that it was a sign of weakness to admit to mental and emotional difficulties. But right then I was feeling so desperate for help that I took his advice and went to a therapist.

Within ten minutes she diagnosed me as clinically depressed. I poured out all my history of struggle and depression to her, and she nodded sympathetically and gave me lots of professional advice. But when I left her office I felt even worse than before I went in. I told myself that that's not supposed to be the result of seeing a therapist – I should be feeling better, not feeling worse.

I went back a few days later but with the same results. I could tell that talk therapy wasn't going to help me. I was just too far gone. I knew what I wanted, what I desperately needed – I needed to just get totally away from everything in my personal life, get myself out and away from this entire American culture that seemed to have entirely consumed my soul. I just couldn't take any of it anymore.

All during this time, I kept remembering how good and free and alive and 'me' I'd felt when I'd been off traveling in another country, totally away from the chronic work buzz of American civilization. For over twenty years now, I'd been trying to prove that I could fit into this manic-paced hyper-competitive culture that my parents had brought me into. And this was where I'd ended up? From my overwhelmed perspective, life itself did seem totally hopeless. I was finally entirely worked out, feeling that I'd been squeezed down into abject nothingness and then left a hopeless wreck engulfed in agonizing emptiness. I know this sounds overly melodramatic, but from the inside out that's what I was caught up in right then.

A few days later Arkady returned home after a work trip – and I just spontaneously exploded as soon as we were alone together. I felt something primal snap between us and break. I became suddenly entirely disconnected from him, I didn't care about his feelings at all anymore. I realized that I was already gone in my heart.

I told him quite bluntly that I was leaving, that I was jumping on the next plane back to Vietnam for at least a few weeks and hey, maybe forever. I wasn't promising anything, I was just leaving. Period. Goodbye. End of discussion. That was that – I didn't care what he thought. I just knew that it was time for me to really break away from Arkady and his whole world, and do it for real this time.

I didn't think any of this through, I just vomited everything up at him and dropped my entire load on his head. He would quite suddenly have to step in and take full responsibility for the kids, he'd have to stop traveling and stay with them – because I was out! Not even my parents could change my mind, they were of zero help to me right then. I was leaving them finally too. In fact I was already gone.

And so yes, I left. I was being utterly selfish, totally retreating into a protective cocoon – because otherwise I knew I was going to do something horrific, I was going to kill myself … and thus retreat forever. I remember walking numbly into the interior of the jet headed to Hong Kong and Saigon, sitting there with a totally blank mind as I flew up and off and away. And I can also remember how, many hours later with America far behind me, I step by step began to feel as if I was somehow miraculously coming alive somewhere deep inside.

By the time I landed in Saigon and caught a bus, my inner mood had evolved into a state of silent calmness. There were almost no thoughts flowing through my mind, no recollections of my past, no anticipations of any future. I was just there in a bumpy bus that was taking me back in time to my grandparents' home, my old family village on the Mekong.

My life had clearly gone full circle – leaving a devastated war zone as an infant refugee, arriving in the promised land, surviving and finally thriving – and now here I was, returning home to my native source as a sad-case psychologically-traumatized refugee urgently escaping from that promised land.

I found myself once again entering a supposedly-primitive culture with almost none of the supposed necessities of modern life. This was exactly what I'd been hungering for – a safe simple place where I could finally come to a full stop … and relax! I'd left everything behind in Boston. I now had nothing but I had everything I needed. I had inner calm and I felt satisfied, safe, content to just be. Immersed in the surrounding simplicity of rural Vietnamese life, I felt like I'd actually escaped death itself. And probably that was very close to the truth.

My grandparents welcomed me with open arms and almost no questions. I think they could sense that I wasn't my normal self and so they gave me all the space I needed. I fell thankfully asleep that night and was awakened the next morning by roosters announcing the new day. Outside, the tall upright palm trees were swaying in the warm breeze. I realized that I had absolutely nothing to do, nowhere to go, no one at all demanding anything of me.

As I lay with my eyes closed in a hammock tied between two coconut trees, I could hear the grunting noises of the pigs my uncle was raising, and now and then in the distance I heard the roar of a motorbike driving by. I felt a calm come over me that was just exquisite. I felt no stress at all, I was free, I'd escaped! I wasn't going to kill myself.

The depression that had been consuming me simply dissolved and evaporated from my innards. My heart felt it was being lovingly soothed and healed by the morning sun rising over the Pacific Ocean, breathing fresh life into my soul as everything from my American yesterdays disappeared, eclipsed by the purifying rays of a bright new day. It's impossible to really describe such feelings without sounding trite – but this was the opposite of trite. Being able to breathe freely again truly felt like I was being reborn.

There was barely any internet connection in the village, at least that I knew of, and I didn't want to connect with Arkady or my parents anyway. Everyone back there in crazy America, even my children, would simply have to get by on their own – I'd given them my all for as long as I could. Now I'd relinquished all my responsibilities. And yes – it felt remarkably good to be so selfish!

In retrospect I guess I was just finally caring for my own self, for the first time in a long time. My shoulders felt light and relieved of all the responsibilities, many of them self-imposed, that had been weighing me down. As the next few days flowed gently by, I began to experience a remarkable new sense of happiness or some even-deeper inner quality of contentment. Just the simple sensory experience of being here back home in an outdoor hammock – this was exactly where I needed to be, where I deserved to be right now in my life.

As my physical energy returned I started fully enjoying myself. My relatives were happy to be my hosts and care for me. I went around here and there on foot to visit family, and I ate their good everyday food … and didn't get sick. I became stronger in all ways. I still have no idea what was really happening inside me, it was all mostly unconscious. This sense of spontaneous inner healing certainly wasn't therapy, I wasn't working through all my mental hang-ups and emotional problems and all the rest. I just … let it all go. Something surrendered inside me. I gave up … and at least at some levels, yes, I healed.

I perhaps should be able to say more about this process. Sometimes I think I was working through my parents' stuff. Sometimes I think I was breaking free of those college years at Bowdoin when I got locked so tightly into a false career path driven by a distorted sense of what it means to succeed. All I know is that by returning to where I started, something came full circle inside me – and for that to happen, I simply had to at least temporarily turn my back on everything I'd become, and tune into the deeper vibes of my origins.

Whatever it was, this return home marked a turning point in my life. I gave up thinking that I carried the world on my shoulders – that was too much to sustain. I'll always be deeply thankful to my instincts, to my readiness to follow my gut urge to get the hell out. Otherwise I would have sunk into a quagmire of endless therapy sessions and depressing depression pills – or worse.

And so it came to pass that, after around two weeks of total freedom and the soothing sense of having made good my escape, I knew my retreat was over. I wasn't destined to return permanently to live the life of my ancestors. For a few days my focus of attention gently began to shift on its own beyond this local present-moment world, and my thoughts and also my heart opened again to my children, to Arkady, to my family back in America – and even to the work I'd so suddenly left behind. Besides, the weather was really terribly hot in Vietnam that time of year.

My time in Asia didn't end in Vietnam. I decided to fly from Saigon to Hong Kong and spend a good week with Naeem and Mehvesh who were living there at the time. I knew the weather would be cooler and less humid farther north – and the idea of flying into Hong Kong and enjoying the comforts of modern civilization again began to grow inside me. That would be a good transition back into reality.

The day I was leaving Vietnam I found myself getting up with a lot of energy and eagerness as I said goodbyes to my Vietnam family and then made my way by bus to the Tan San Nhut airport and from there flew up to Hong Kong. When I got there, sharing a few days with Naeem and Mehvesh, they helped me remember and feel thankful for all the good times I'd had along every step of my journey.

I could never really say how, but mostly subconsciously I managed in my heart to bridge all my disparate worlds together – Vietnam, Seattle, Los Angeles, Lawrence, Bowdoin, Paris, Princeton, New York, Washington D.C., Africa, the Middle East and most recently, my current Boston home and community. I was finally able to really appreciate my experiences despite all the curveballs that life had thrown at me.

The island of Hong Kong offered me two different worlds to escape into – the modern buzz of a luxurious coastal city-state, and the near-pristine mountains and steep hills surrounding the city. Mehvesh took me into her favorite city haunts, reminding me of all the good things found in city living. Naeem took me up into the mountains to share some of the serenity and happiness found only in nature. Their love and acceptance, when I told them all I'd been going through, was a final healing balm given as a beautiful gift before I headed back home to family and work and whatever my future might hold.

Chapter Twenty

~~~~~~~~~~~~~~~~~~~~~~~~~~~~

While I was enjoying my much-needed healing break from my family, Arkady back home had been struggling to take care of the kids. Before I'd left and forced him to assume that responsibility, he'd often said that his job out in the business world was obviously harder than my job raising the kids – but he found out otherwise. Even with the support of both pairs of parents, he discovered what I'd been almost desperately struggling with – running a household and working at the same time.

When I came back to Boston I felt entirely rejuvenated. I didn't know what to expect from Ark, but I myself had gone through a definite change in my attitude and life expectations. I wasn't going to just drop back into my former routines. I was going to actively choose how my life would unfold from here on out.

And Ark surprised me. I guess he finally realized my worth. He now seemed to see me differently because he related to me in a new way – in fact he appeared to have made a 180-degree turn. He started treating me almost exactly like I'd always been dreaming of – he became his unique version of my Cary Grant. Our marriage improved, and so did our attitude toward parenting. He helped a lot more, and he openly appreciated how I ran the household.

And for myself, I felt much more open to my full role as the mother of my daughter and my son. Somehow, without any overt
~~~~~~~~~~~~~~~~~~~~~~~~~~~~

decisions or actions, our family came into focus. Ark as usual didn't really articulate any reasons for his change of heart toward me. But he did admit that, before I left for Vietnam, he hadn't realized how hard it was to be me, to be in that position of assuming full responsibility for the entire household and at the same time working so hard.

I also think that Ark realized I was right on the brink of really leaving him. And at deeper levels, he also seemed to wake up to how much he loved me, and how he wanted to express that feeling of love more. He told me he could now see how I'd given up my career for our family, and how in the last few years I'd also dedicated myself to helping him build his company. After I came back from Vietnam he was fully supportive of everything I decided to get involved in.

I immediately left his company but rather than looking for another job, I began exploring my own journey. My driving passion in life had somehow become the entrepreneurial process of building companies. My first attempts either failed or didn't succeed at high levels – but I steadily experimented and began to figure out how startups functioned. My self-confidence grew and I took more risks, stepping further out of my shell and overcoming aspects of business that I'd always been afraid of.

What was most difficult for me was talking to people about funding my projects. I had to learn how to sell – and that meant first of all, learning how to sell myself, to feel confident and openly believe in my budding projects. My former boss Victoria had once assured me that if I was ever given the chance to assume leadership roles, she was confident I'd be able to succeed – but up until now I hadn't been given that chance. Now the opportunity, the challenge was present – and luckily Arkady in his new attitude toward me was supportive, readily offering both his encouragement and his coaching.

At first I thought I could start a business on my own without funding, and avoid that whole issue. I had a prejudice against people who were fixated on money. They were in an entirely different socio-economic group than I was, they were a different type of beast. They certainly weren't people I could speak easily with. On one occasion when I started to explore raising money, I tried to gently do my pitch to a potential investor – but he later sat down with me and said, "Mai, you are too nice. Nice people don't succeed."

On another occasion I sat in a room trying to pitch to a guy who kept on looking at the clock on his wall as I was talking. I should have stopped my pitch and left – but I was nice, I didn't want to be rude. Finally I was done and I left. He sent me an email rejecting my proposal and he said the same thing – that I was too nice.

Raising money sucked! I loved everything else about building companies. For a while I continued trying to build software companies without raising money, using our family savings and whatever I could borrow. And as it so often happens, I stumbled by chance into a new startup concept. I was always clipping coupons back then, and I couldn't keep track of them all.

I wanted to somehow keep that information on my phone, and I thought maybe other people would like to do that too. So I went to work building that software with a developer. But that type of software was a bit ahead of its time – people couldn't quite get the idea of taking pictures of their coupons. However, several stores asked if I could put their products on the app, so I did as they requested.

I kept following new ways to expand the app, adding things like the Farmers Market in my town of Brookline, just west of Boston. Then I realized I could expand another notch and link up restaurants and high-end produce stores with all the truck farmers and local commercial fishermen, handling wonderful fresh produce that needed to get into the city fast and predictably.

At first the farmers I approached out on their farms told me that they loved the traditional ways of bringing produce to market – but I kept on going back to them, I wasn't afraid of farmers like I was of investors. I felt a kinship with those hardworking, straightforward, no-frills people who were just doing their best to make it through life.

Meanwhile I kept working really hard on the basic concept of bringing all players in the 'farm to table' loop together via tech. I worked quite well with programmers and learned how to build websites, mastering all the technical dimensions – and finally one farmer finally said, "Well okay I'll give you a try."

I did everything to prove that my system was worth her trust. I was able to help her expand her revenue – and then word got around and I started adding other farmers. I expanded beyond Farmers Markets and started working with restaurants who wanted to connect daily with those same farmers. This quickly became very successful, I began working with high-end restaurants.

But the delivery dimension of my budding system was often not performing on time, and I found myself having to do a lot of deliveries myself. So in another expansion I added a delivery team. I was on a roll, things were expanding fast – but still I refused to ask for investment money.

I must admit that I became so caught up in this new company that I wasn't paying enough attention to my family. I did everything required physically for my household but, just like my parents had, I was again working non-stop. I cooked and cleaned and so forth in the house. And that was how I expressed my love to my children, rather than easing up and spending fun loving time with them.

Looking back, I can now see that I wanted my children to be raised with the same values, attitudes and family atmosphere I'd been raised in – that same constantly-struggling refugee atmosphere. I thought I had to teach them tenacity and toughness, not softness and love. I wanted them to appreciate hard work and I definitely didn't want them to grow up snobbish. Basically I wanted them to carry on our Vietnamese family traditions. I think I unconsciously assumed that all this was expected of me by my own parents.

But of course we were now living in a very different environment. We had saved and bought a nice home in Brookline – the exact opposite of the 'hoods' I'd lived in during my own formative childhood days. In so many ways, Arkady and I were giving our children an entirely different experience than what we grew up with. My kids were living a vastly more privileged life, they weren't refugees or immigrants at all.

But still I reflexively tried to imbed in Leah various elements of that refugee life. For instance I didn't give her little-girl toys to play with. She really wanted an American girl doll with white skin but I thought that was entirely pointless, spending money on something like that when we could spend it on food or books – even though such small sums of money were no longer an issue at all.

I'd never had the chance to have books and delve into reading when I was young, and I wanted Leah to value such opportunities. I gave her all sorts of practical resources but I held firm and didn't give her certain playthings to live out her own unique childhood. And the result? Even when she was very young we banged heads continually, she cried a lot and threw terrible tantrums.

I do feel guilty for how I acted back then. After all, Leah was generally bright and often hilarious, she was very smart and naturally cute – but I didn't adequately appreciate those wonderful dimensions of her budding personality. Even back then as a very young girl, she noticed that I was quite harsh on her compared to how the mothers of her friends in school treated their daughters.

Leah's tantrums often became so unbearable that I got pushed way beyond my limits. I don't know how much gets passed on generation after generation in this regard, but I do know that I cried terribly as an infant – and now my daughter was throwing tantrums that I couldn't control or hardly bear. So what could I do? I pushed for her to receive some professional therapy, even before she was attending kindergarten.

We started going to a therapist together and somehow this seemed to help. She talked openly with the therapist and it seemed that progress was being made. Then suddenly she didn't need to go anymore. Her tantrums had become manageable, so we stopped the therapy. But I decided to continue with therapy myself, to perhaps learn how to become a better mom.

My conflicts with Leah continued. She seemed to feel that I didn't really love her, that I had no time for her. And I must admit that this was at least partly true. As I mentioned earlier, I was mostly consumed in my work. Ever since I went to college and then started all my various jobs, I'd become compulsive about work. Leah would say, "Why did you even have me if all you care about is work?"

I know that I can't take back or erase how I was with Leah. I simply wasn't able to force myself to feel that strong maternal connection that she yearned for. I'm trying to open up to that level of feelings with her now, but is it too late? It took me far too long to realize that, hey, I need to grow, I need to change myself inside, ease up and create space in my heart to express love in my family. I can't force Leah to be me. I can't force her to be someone or something that she's not. Mothering shouldn't involve that kind of mammary manipulation.

However, from an early age Leah seemed especially smart, and that was something I could readily support. I tried to get her special enrichment resources in the public school she was attending but nothing came of my efforts. I was brought up in public schools and believed in them – but Leah became more and more frustrated with her education, she was super sharp in math and science and wasn't being challenged at all.

In fourth grade she asked me politely, "Do you think I can apply to a private girl's school?" And I told her, "No, you cannot. You're not going to a private school. That's elitist, that's not us. You're staying in public school, that's why we moved to this suburb – because it has such good public schools."

But she continued asking me, coming up with arguments to convince me, saying, "Look, I'll just apply, most likely I won't get in, and I'll do it all on my own." Her fourth-grade teacher was supportive of this, telling me that she believed Leah would do well in the private school she was focused on, if she could get in. I was still against the whole idea but I assumed Leah wouldn't be accepted because it's a very selective school. So I allowed her to apply.

I ultimately had to help her with the application but I hated every moment of it. I would get angry and shout at her that we could never afford the tuition, that the whole idea was ridiculous. I told her the private school was full of nothing but rich kids, that she would become spoiled. I seriously didn't want to see her inserted into that kind of environment – it reminded me too much of the rich Bowdoin kids who had rejected me. I wanted Leah to appreciate who we were, how our families had struggled. I thought it was important for her to connect to real people in regular schools, not rich kids in their exclusive bubble.

But she applied anyway, and as parents Ark and I were invited in for an interview. Arkady to this day insists that he almost had to drag me out of the meeting because I argued so much with the admissions officer, asking questions like "Why should my daughter even go to this school, what's so special about it? It's not diverse, it's only white and Asian."

As Arkady and I walked out of the interview I was rejoicing. "Oh, I think I did a good job, she's not going to get in there." When we got home and told Leah it had been a difficult interview, she was of course both sad and angry at me for not putting on my best self to help her. Then March rolled around and we got an email from the school with its decision – and the first thing that came out of my mouth was: "Oh, fuck!"

I decided to tell Leah that she got in, that she did great, applying mostly on her own – but sorry, we simply couldn't afford it. But when I told her she'd been accepted, and saw how happy she was, I didn't have the heart to tell her she couldn't go. Instead I phoned a friend who worked at Harvard, asking for advice on what to do with Leah. He told me that, with her bright mind and her early eagerness to push forward with her education, she definitely deserved the private school opportunity. He knew my background and reminded me that my parents had done so much to get me a better education, they'd sacrificed everything for me – so perhaps I should do the same for my daughter and find a way to afford the tuition.

I was still upset when I hung up. I can now see that I was quite prejudiced against the kind of people who send their kids to elite schools. I never hang out with them, I just don't fit in – but I had to give in and let Leah go there. But I refused to take her shopping for fancy school clothes. She'd at least have to stay humble and real at that level, and wear whatever she already had.

So off she went to private school every morning, surrounded by wealthy kids who had everything – and my relationship with Leah remained physically restrictive. I wanted her to be grounded. I felt she needed to understand the dire history of her family in order for her to really appreciate life. Then at some point my therapist patiently pointed out that yes, I'd struggled early in my life but I wasn't struggling so much anymore – and furthermore, my past struggles weren't my daughter's struggles. She'd have her own struggles to deal with in her life, so why was I trying to force my past struggles onto her?

My therapist was right of course. And I started to let Leah buy things she wanted. I tried to change my attitude and to see that I personally seemed to thrive on the challenge of constantly struggling, perhaps I was someone who needed perpetual struggle in order to feel that I had value in the world – but I didn't need to force others to relate to life that way.

Chapter Twenty-One

~~~~~~~~~~~~~~~~~~~~~~~~~~~~~~~~~~~~

During this time on the career front I became more confident in my role as an Asian-American woman running startups. I used to feel good about making money but guilty about spending money, especially buying nonessential things. But after my Vietnam trip something changed. I began to realize that hey, the past was over. I had evolved and matured, and I had a right to live a good life in the present moment.

I was also starting to embrace my daughter's life – like, she is who she is, she is not me, she's developing her own sense of self – and she deserves and simply must be free to explore her own uniqueness. She wasn't born on a Vietnam riverbank, she was born at a hospital in Washington D.C. My challenge was to find ways to share with her my deeper values without forcing them on her. We all have to discover our own values, our own sense of what life is all about.

In general, with help from my therapist, I began to be more observant of how I was affecting the people around me. I started to be more cognizant that we all have a responsibility to set our own selves free – and at the same time we must set others free to decide what values, attitudes and goals they want to embrace in their lives.
~~~~~~~~~~~~~~~~~~~~~~~~~~~~~~~~~~~~

I was also struggling to understand and accept Arkady's dad's attitudes and prejudices. When he'd declared when Ark and I got married that he didn't want any yellow grandchildren, that comment had of course struck me to the quick at the time, and put a gigantic barrier between us – but when I'd come back to Boston with my newborn daughter, I'd felt it was essential to somehow bring our immigrant Vietnamese-Russian family together.

So I'd regularly made an effort to start opening my heart and home to Arkady's parents and family. I physically expressed this sentiment by giving his parents a set of our house keys when we moved from my parents' home into our apartment. I told them they were welcome to come visit any time – and also when they needed something, I'd be happy to go and get it for them.

At first they didn't much respond, they seemed hesitant to be close to me and the baby. They didn't often offer to help us with Leah. But they were both working full time, they didn't have much energy left to help. I didn't allow their reticence to stop me from doing things for them. I started hosting big family gatherings for holidays like Thanksgiving and birthdays, taking the lead in getting presents, throwing surprise Mother's Day and birthday parties for Arkady's mother. I'd buy her presents and say they were from Arkady.

I was also regularly helping Arkady's grandmother. She was a remarkable human being, encouraging her grandchildren to open their minds and hearts to everyone around them. She had suffered greatly and could have ended up as a depressed hateful person. Most of her family had died in the Holocaust and she'd lived most of her life without hardly anything. Then in her old age in Boston, when she needed something her grandsons were almost always not available to help her. So I was the one who'd run over and bring her groceries, visit her regularly, keep her company. I'm not implying that I did all of this out of the goodness of my heart, although I did feel good when I helped her. I was driven by my underlying urge to somehow make our extended family feel united and harmonious.

And over time Ark's family did begin to be warmer and to open up to my side of the family. In fact after a while they wanted to see us all the time. They actually wanted to be an active part of our lives, even though our two families were so utterly different in culture, religion, food, customs and all the rest.

The most satisfying development for me and Ark during the years after Leah's birth was that my parents and his parents really came to care about each other. Then when we had our son, Elan, Arkady's parents fully opened up. They'd just retired at that time, so they began caring for Elan almost every workday, becoming his primary caretakers.

Also I decided to raise our children with many Jewish elements in their upbringing. Leah and Elan have both been learning Hebrew as a language. And Leah had her bat mitzvah in Israel – a small ceremony, nothing lavish, but quite meaningful. And we celebrate every Jewish holiday. I myself haven't converted, but I'm supportive.

The other gesture I made, along with agreeing to move back to Boston when we got married, was to change my last name to Ark's. In Vietnam, women don't change their names, they use their maiden names all their lives. But I agreed to please Arkady on that point.

So … I guess mine is yet another story of the great American melting pot. A transcultural marriage certainly takes time to find its own ground, and you have to be willing to take an amazing leap. At least one person must be willing to compromise, to stick to the effort until others in the family realize that letting go, and coming together in a new way – that this is the American way. Otherwise, as is all too common, mixed immigrant unions tend to end in tragedy.

I haven't said much about my mother here. I did mention that she was very quiet, that she adhered to her tradition of women being submissive and even subservient. Before the war she grew up quite wealthy, my grandfather was a big landowner. After that, she pretty much lived in poverty. I've been told by relatives that she was very unassuming, never wearing much makeup or jewelry and never talking negatively about people.

She told me her war memories of working in the fields somewhere north of where she grew up. There was ongoing bombing for entire months, and she had to help dig trenches and a tunnel to escape being blown up. They were finally reduced to eating rodents and whatever they could find, just to stave off starvation. She had been separated from the rest of her family, she really lost everything, she dropped all the way down to just raw survival levels.

Because of the war she got married in her late twenties, which is late for a Vietnamese woman. My dad was a really good-looking young man with his curly hair and chiseled cheeks. I'm told that a lot of women were after him, but he went for my mom. They were married and I was born. After the war, like I mentioned before, the Viet Cong were looking for men who'd worked with the U.S. military. So my dad often had to run and hide, and both before and after I was born, they were always moving around.

I now realize that even in the womb, I was immersed in my mom's anxious emotions provoked by that extreme situation. My mom holds everything inside, she doesn't really express herself, she just takes whatever comes her way and tries to be happy with that. If she didn't have food for a day, she wouldn't get upset. But I assume she did experience terrible amounts of trauma, both before and after we arrived in America.

When we came to America, survival-wise Mom carried with her what she'd learned back home. She would always cook exactly what we needed to eat and no more. She would never waste. And she never bought anything for herself. She still takes our old clothes and repurposes them for herself. And when we buy something for her, she saves it – we have to force her to get it out and wear it or use it. My dad does the same thing.

In reflection, with each new generation the females of my family have been getting more confident and powerful. My mom doesn't come off as a confident person but she did get out and get a good job in America. And I myself, as her child, didn't feel at all confident initially. But then over time I was able to build up my self-confidence, because I found myself in situations where I was permitted and even encouraged to do so.

And yes, I've certainly raised my daughter to feel confident, and Ark's tradition is strong in that realm as well. But also I've hoped to instill the meek, virtuous and sincere qualities of my mom, even though those are qualities that people take advantage of. When she started working in the post office, Mom barely spoke English and was overeager to please. She is too nice!!! The investor was right – nice people don't win. And so she ended up working through all the holidays even though she didn't get paid more – and she didn't receive pay increases because she never asked for them. She was just happy and appreciative that she had a job.

Leah is the opposite. When Arkady asked her to work in his office, she insisted on getting paid the same as he paid other older people doing the same work. She presented her arguments vigorously, insisting on fairness – and in the end she got it.

Looking back over my life, I can see why I developed my workaholic habit, or even compulsion. I was so focused on surviving. The feeling of there not being enough time in the day to get everything done is so ingrained in me. The challenge we all face in life is letting go of old attitudes and habits when they no longer serve us – but that's easier said than done, to say the least.

My dad came to America with no skills that would pay him hardly anything at all, so when we got to Massachusetts he realized he had to both work and also study at the same time, to somehow get ahead. He went to community college night classes to learn how to be a technician. Then he worked at different jobs, whatever was available – where he often got hit with racial slurs and put-downs and even worse.

I remember when I was twelve, he was so excited to get a new job where he was one of just a few Asian technicians. He was able to help the company improve its production process, he was an asset – but he still didn't speak English very well, and some of his colleagues didn't like him for one reason or another. One day he was in the lunch room and one of his colleagues came in and pulled out his penis with a yellow condom on it – and started shouting racial swears at my dad.

Dad didn't say a single thing in response. He just took the abuse. But he quit the company because of that. He took the high road and remained silent to avoid confrontation. A few days later there was a knock on our door. I went to open it and found two white men who wanted to talk to my dad. They said that on behalf of the company they apologized for the pain caused to my family. But then the company went on like nothing had happened – and my dad didn't have a job.

My mom's response was never to let such things visibly upset her. She said it was just the way life was in America. She assumed we'd never become a part of American society, so she just accepted whatever was given to us. She didn't ask for more – she didn't want to cause any more problems. Also I think she was still very traumatized by the refugee camps, by not having enough food to eat – and always being afraid of someone attacking us.

But as the next generation after my parents, I simply cannot accept such simplicity and acceptance of all the injustices in the world. My attitude has been hard for my parents to wrestle with, and a point of tension in our relationship. They don't want me to disrupt what I've gained – but sometimes I need to disrupt! I need to break free and speak my own mind.

Unfortunately in our world, in this country and even within my groups of family and friends, differing views are often not tolerated. Our ongoing problem is that so many of us are caught up in self-righteousness, in defending our own views and angrily denying other views, that we continually poison the very same heart feelings we so hunger for.

FINAL WORDS

~~~~~~~~~~~~~~~~

Now
~~~~~~~~~~~~~~~~

Chapter Twenty-Two

My father was naturally disappointed when I suddenly got pregnant and came crashing out of my projected future at the World Bank or a related top-tier occupation. I obviously didn't plan that exit, becoming a mother was the last thing on my mind down in D.C. But it happened, and my life evolved – and my occupational passions shifted as a consequence.

As I mentioned earlier, my business focus after D.C. began to evolve from wanting to be part of a big organization in a nine-to-five employee position, to hungering for the more-adventurous work of a free-wheeling independent entrepreneur. Ark had gone in that direction, I'd worked in his growing company – and then I wanted to do something myself. I really wanted to build something of my own. I wanted to step outside what was expected of me, take Victoria's sage advice and assume my own leadership roles and business destiny.

I first of all had managed to let go entirely of being involved in Arkady's business. We had some savings that I could draw from – and as I described earlier, I quite naturally fell into the idea of helping farmers and fishermen get their fresh produce quickly and profitably to market.

Part of the rush of the entrepreneurial experience is how taking one step just spontaneously tends to lead to the next step. I happened to meet a Princeton-trained engineer who was pretty fabulous, and he offered to work with me building any sort of software system I might need. Soon we were focusing on a digital system to help farmers negotiate all their producer-consumer transactions.

We also designed an app to coordinate the movement of fresh goods from field and sea to the awaiting city of Boston. The original 'coupon idea' morphed into using new tech to support farmers and fishermen deliver their goods fast and predictably to local markets and restaurants. I just loved that warm feeling that I felt doing this work, the inner sense of being of genuine help to people who were struggling to keep their farms profitable as they helped feed our local city with healthy goods.

During this time most people I knew thought I had a fun hobby of some sort, that I wasn't really working at a job. It looked like I was just living off of Arkady. They were right in some ways. I had let go of any sort of regular employment in order to build my dream, but of course I had also, several years earlier, given up my earlier career in order to run a household and support Arkady.

He and I shared the subtle feeling of an invisible balance in our work lives that most people didn't see. His friends just thought I had carte blanche to do whatever I wanted, and I often seemed to be just hanging out chatting with people, making new friends out in the country – and of course, being a housewife. I remember an acquaintance came up to me in the street one day and said, "Oh, so how's your hobby doing?"

The truth was the opposite. I hardly slept at night, I worked seven days a week. When I managed to fit in a vacation, I always had my laptop with me. I was a solo entrepreneur for a while, except during the time Sagi joined, with no investor. I didn't take any money from anyone. I used only our limited savings, even though this type of business would normally require fundraising. I attempted to do that on a few occasions but it just totally turned me off.

But lack of investors didn't deter me from pursuing my dream. I found an alternative to raising money. My business partner, Sagi, and I built the business and platform that drove the whole project. And rather than hiring employees to do the physical runaround work, I decided to go out myself and get customers signed up, then work out delivery systems as I went along.

When it came to signing farmers and fishermen into our system, for a couple months I got nothing but rejections. Then finally I got some tentative 'maybe' responses and after that things got going. I harassed people enough to where finally one person, Kate from Stillman Quality Meats, said, "Okay, let's talk." I told her, "Look, just give me a chance to show you what I can do." She did … and I did.

I helped her set up new restaurant and retail accounts, and we became friends in the process. Then other farmers started coming on board, and also restaurants who were hungry for fresher dependable produce deliveries. I set up transportation teams and cut out storage and waste. Produce went straight from farm to restaurant. Everyone was pleased. Chickens were butchered the night before they were cooked in a restaurant's kitchen – and I had all these wonderful chefs giving me more orders. As things progressed we did quite well, even though there were times when we wondered if it would all collapse.

Too often, family arguments revolved around my working all the time on my business while also trying to deal with too much around the house – fixing doors, gardening, cooking, cleaning. I did our taxes, paid our bills. Arkady didn't touch any of that. And I was also very reluctant to outsource any jobs in my business.

Meanwhile a chef named Mario Batali was launching a unique Italian-themed shopping 'village', Eataly, in Boston. They started using my services, ordering more and more from my farmers, who were working around the clock trying to pick and also deliver so many farm-fresh orders.

Our overall success was now feeling palpable – but both the logistics and the supply chain soon became unsustainable. Without a cold-storage space we were doing everything literally from farm direct to table. The farms initially took the responsibility to deliver to restaurants and stores, I just coordinated. But too often the farmers couldn't handle the deliveries and so I had to step in.

I remember one Thanksgiving when I personally had to deliver a load of fresh turkey carcasses – and returned home covered in turkey blood to jump in and cook my own Thanksgiving feast. Also, Arkady would often get embarrassed walking in public with me dressed completely disheveled, smelling like fish rather than a sophisticated entrepreneur – but hey, pragmatically I had to wear clothes I could get dirty or bloody or whatever.

One day while out helping make a delivery, I bent down and my jeans ripped right in the middle of my butt crack. I walked around the whole day like that not bothered at all. I really loved my work, I felt like I was becoming a needed and valued part of our local farming community. They were people I could quite naturally connect with. I didn't have to prove anything, I could just be myself.

This was a truly wonderful and liberating feeling! I definitely didn't want to be flashy with the farmers, so I drove my Subaru when I was working with them. Driving along back roads into farms, I felt comfortable in a vehicle that was humble – it was more than willing to pack a bunch of farm-fresh produce into the back seat and trunk.

And then – I got pregnant with my third child, and everything changed. Parallel to how my attitude shifted in D.C. at the World Bank, becoming pregnant shifted my entire sense of who I was and what satisfied me. I began to lose my passionate interest in the order/delivery coordination business I'd devoted the last several years of my life to. I'd proven that I could take a startup all the way onto solid ground. And now – I wasn't feeling so excited about the work anymore. It had become such a big headache of a logistics business.

On the last day of 2017 I was almost eight months pregnant, we had a big order to deliver for New Year's Eve – and there was a major storm. The farm simply couldn't get the order out on time and there was no delivery help available, so I had to get up steam and go do the delivery myself. I remember feeling truly exhausted, like I just couldn't carry on anymore – but the delivery had to be made.

Arkady saw my dilemma, and he insisted that I was too pregnant to lift any heavy loads. So he came along with me on the delivery run – and he was astonished to see first-hand just how physically difficult and inefficient my system was. He insisted right then that I had to stop my work. And … I agreed. There was just no way I could continue with this heavy work load and also give birth and mother my new baby.

So right away I gave in and started to pull away from my business. After my son was born on February 14th, I announced to all my farmers and customers that I was stopping my service. I didn't really have the capacity or drive or funding to hire a team and figure out logistics with me disappearing from the operation. There was no choice but to just let it go – but ending the business was really hard. I didn't want to feel that I was a failure, but I didn't have the drive to go out and try to sell the business. So I just closed it down.

My ever-lurking sense of depression sometimes pulled me down, but a big part of me felt really satisfied. I had learned so much, and been of service, regardless of how difficult the work had been. I'd had a great journey – but this was the end of that journey. When I gave birth to my third son, I decided to take a full year off from any new project, and not do anything work-wise. Then I'd figure out my next gig.

People close to me said they didn't believe I could take a year off, that I wasn't the type of person to just sit around and do nothing. And they were right – when opportunity came knocking at my door a few months later, asking me to come on board and run a new startup venture … I said yes. I'd proven that I was passionate about projects I took on, and that I was willing to get my hands dirty. I wasn't one of those execs looking for a cerebral job, that's not what startups are all about. I was eager to get back to work.

Chapter Twenty-Three

~~~~~~~~~~~~~~~~~~~~~~~~~~~~~~~~~~~

But there's something besides business and babies that I need to talk about before I end this account. I want to share my experiences regarding a universal forbidden topic that almost all of us confront at least a few times in our lives – but that we're taught to feel ashamed of, to hide away, to somehow deal with on our own. Perhaps my own story will be of help if I can be open and honest.

The first time I felt suicidal impulses was back in college. I'd never had those thoughts or urges prior to college. I really loved living up until then, even as hard as those early years had been. The rough-and-tumble neighborhoods and all the constant hardships of Seattle, SoCal and Lawrence had simply seemed normal to me. Even days when my parents didn't know where money would come from to buy us food, things always worked out, we didn't ever starve or end up out in the street.

So I felt all through childhood like life was good. I went to bed, I dreamed, I woke up and had my routines that I went through during the day. Emotionally I felt mostly strong and okay, I felt bright inside. Times only got tough for me emotionally and mentally when I left everything I'd known and went off to college.

It wasn't Bowdoin in particular, it probably could have been any college. Suddenly I was separated from my family and neighborhood friends. I didn't know who I was in this new social
~~~~~~~~~~~~~~~~~~~~~~~~~~~~~~~~~~~

environment, and I got hit with the devastating feeling of not belonging – of being lost. I could feel no connection to anything around me. Worse still, I also somehow felt entirely disconnected from my own self.

The various philosophers I read in college call what I was feeling the dark night of the soul. The French existentialists I explored were especially fixated on this blank darkness. The immense weight in my chest wasn't exactly pain or hurt, I just felt that I couldn't stand being where I was inside my own head and heart, inside my own skin. But – I found out that there was no way to run away from this terrible feeling. The only way out that I could see, at least in the darkest episodes of my depression, was to somehow escape by ending it all.

I couldn't go to my parents. They would just tell me to buck up and be strong. And I couldn't imagine talking with anyone on campus about what I was agonizingly stuck in. How could I even begin to describe this invisible horror, people would think I'd gone crazy. Back then I literally didn't have words to describe my feelings. I'd just suddenly have random tears coming down my cheeks even though I had no overt reason to be crying. I couldn't explain why I was sobbing, I simply felt there was no way out except to disappear from the face of the Earth – permanently.

Of course, I didn't feel like this all the time at Bowdoin, I had many good times, as I talked about earlier. I had friends who delighted me and kept me laughing for hours. I had thrills about learning something entirely new. I had wonderful sexual times and jogging times and dreaming times … but then the darkness would sneak up on me and grab me – and I'd be plunged again into the pits.

When that heavy darkness grabbed me, it felt like those depressed feelings would never ever end. I knew from experience that if I could only make it through to the next day, I'd probably feel better. But in the middle of a bout of depression it was impossible to imagine a better tomorrow – I felt lost in a torture chamber of the eternal now. I could grasp no hope to hold onto, no light at the end of the proverbial tunnel.

By the way, many times when the darkness began to grab me, Arkady would be there and he'd somehow have the patience and compassion to really be present for me, even if he didn't know what was happening inside me. People do really help – usually. Arkady many times just got me through the night. Then a new day would dawn and I'd be okay for a while.

I think everyone knows the low painful days that are transitory, the deep emotional holes we can all periodically fall into without seeing them coming. I assume this is part of the human condition. It's the price we pay for this big biocomputer in our heads that can think its way into depression, question the purpose of life itself – and push various emotional buttons and hormonal secretions that lead us off into very negative dark places.

But there came times for me in college when those terrible feelings got even worse. They would invade my mindset and grow inside me like an interior monster, becoming so strong that I would not only think about taking my life but also actually think of ways to do it – and then sometimes I'd even begin to act on those impulses. I don't know if you've ever bottomed out that low yourself, or known someone who has. But that's when it gets serious.

Luckily that has happened to me in extremis only on three occasions – and luckily, I was able to snap myself out of my nihilistic state, either because someone physically appeared to break the evil spell, or the helpful thought would pop into my mind that there were people who needed me so much that killing myself would devastate them – and then the lethal impulse would be short-circuited at the last moment.

I won't belabor the actual experiences I moved through in this regard, but I choose to no longer hide them, because they're also part of me. The first time, back at Bowdoin, Arkady was there – he appeared out of the blue as I stood there with the scissors in my hand, and instead of my doing the fatal thing, I burst out crying and collapsed.

The second time I came very close was when I was in D.C. and Arkady suddenly canceled yet another of our pending weddings. I was all alone and the inner agony grew to such proportions that I thought I'd finally had it – I just couldn't handle any more of the emotional torture. I felt I had absolutely nothing to hold onto. The only thing I had was my work. I wasn't that close to my family at that time. I had a few good friends – but I had zero power, zero impulse to reach out to them.

When Ark phoned and canceled the wedding again, I remember feeling like I'd been physically stabbed to death right in the center of my heart – and I just couldn't stand that pain! I collapsed and cried uncontrollably … until I fell asleep. Then I woke up the next morning with puffy eyes and somehow headed off to work.

But a night came when I was suffering so much that my will to keep on living in hell collapsed. I finally gave up entirely.

Grabbing my very-strong migraine pills, I started swallowing them, I took a couple and was ready to take them all – but then something seemingly outside of myself made me pick up the phone and dial my friend Brian. And … just talking to him, admitting openly to someone what was happening, helped. I put down the bottle of pills. I fell asleep. And the next day I woke up and things were somewhat back to normal, the total blackness had eased up again.

I try not to look back or think about those moments when I was so close to ending it all. And I certainly don't share this with hardly anyone. Admitting to suicidal impulses is looked down upon so very judgmentally. If we get honest about what we're going through, we fear that we'll be considered weak, untrustworthy, even crazy. We'll get pushed away as untouchables, perceived as hopelessly over the edge and needing to be locked away somewhere. It seems that suicidal people are far too often feared as having some deadly mental disease that just might be contagious.

When we get hit with some physical illness, or catch a world-wide virus like COVID, we can get medical and emotional support, we're urged to slow down and rest up while the world provides us with the necessary support to recover. My family was hit with COVID and the response of community support was immediate. However, when our souls get attacked there's usually no chicken soup or rest or support for that.

But just like physical health, when our mental health drops down, we can barely carry on performing the basic functions of our daily lives. However, no one wants to be seen that way – so we tend to hide our darkest times, never sharing them or exposing them to the light.

Even though most of us have these dark moments, days, or weeks, we bury them because if we were honest we might lose our job, our friends, even our grip on sanity. But I'm feeling now that sharing my buried experiences definitely seems to help – and I hope my honesty will be of some use in showing that, yes, a normal person can move through these very dark times and yet still continue performing as a responsible, productive and trustworthy member of society.

All of this was especially the case with my third major bout with suicide. This was when I was trying to have a third child, but suffered through a terrible miscarriage that left me utterly bereft. At that time I was also piloting a startup business, taking care of my family with two active kids, and seeing after two pairs of parents. I wasn't submerged in heartbreak, I didn't feel caught in any particular agonizing emotional or existential hurt or pain. But I was definitely riding a non-stop roller coaster of hormonal fluctuations paired with chronic lack of sleep and the seemingly-inherent loneliness and stress of being the founder of a startup and battling my way through the various downsides of entrepreneurship.

Probably no one who hasn't had a miscarriage or death of a child can imagine what that feels like – there's an emptiness, a loneliness, a pathos and grief that's just absolutely terrible. Because of my numerous failed attempts to sustain a pregnancy, I'd lost six children in three years – in fact that was exactly what I'd experienced. But I had to just carry on as if nothing had happened.

Finally it was just too much to take any longer. Once again I'd reached my limits, in fact gone way beyond my limits – so I got in my car and took off fast away from my work, my home, my whole life that had become impossible for me to endure even one moment longer. I don't want to dramatize what happened, but I was very close to just turning the wheel and crashing my car and myself into oblivion forever.

But my mind this time saved me, not anyone on the outside. Well, it was someone on the outside – my two children. Right in the middle of that urgent impulse to crash and burn and be gone, I felt their presence. I felt their need for me to continue living – and that mental and emotional flash of connection snapped me out of the suicidal moment.

As I'm telling you this, I realize that during those three times I came close to taking my life, the feelings were slightly different each time. But what was similar was having my aching feelings entirely overtake my rational mind. I seemed to suddenly slip into an alternate reality of some sort, where there was no way to endure the inner agony even one moment longer. And then luckily, each time something popped me out of that deadly alternate reality.

The choice to end one's life is clearly always present. We are in fact in full charge of our mortal destiny at that ultimate level. And luckily, the life force is very strong. Our primary biological intent is to live as long as we can on this planet! And also, we're social creatures and other people around us can save our lives, literally. Often, they don't even realize what almost happened, nor their role in staving off that possibility.

Is there a higher force, a god by whatever name, who's involved in all this? I think each of us must answer that question for ourselves. Life for me is a mystery that I'm fully immersed in, but not quite comprehending. For me, encounters with the dark night of the soul represent a universal lurking aspect of just being alive as a cognizant human being. From my understanding, such encounters make us stronger, make us more humble, and help us to be more compassionate with others when they're down in the pits.

My dad had such a radically difficult life, as I've shared somewhat in this account. Anyone who has physically fought in a violent war, or been physically threatened in one way or another like being attacked by pirates, they know that the darkest depths of suffering can continue long after the physical abuse and trauma have ended.

But for most of us most of the time, it's not the physical challenges that get to us and push us to the brink – it's the mental and emotional strain and sense of hopelessness that gets to us and sucks us down. And unfortunately, everything we're going through is invisible, it gets blocked, hidden away, not revealed to those around us. Perhaps the worst agony of suicidal impulses is that no one knows what we're going through. We feel so utterly alone.

This is especially true in business. Who wants a CEO who's contemplated suicide? But on the other hand, has anyone ever risen to a high position in a corporation without encountering their own dark night of the soul? However, they can't talk about it or they fear they'd lose their job. Do you really want someone flying your jet airplane who has considered suicide? And how many pilots haven't considered suicide at least once or twice in their lives?

Really – is the stigma of having suicidal thoughts and feelings valid and fair, or should we now rise up as a reasonable compassionate society and begin to more openly deal with this universal human condition? Yes, a number of wonderful organizations are trying to do this, but they need our open support – and that support needs to start with our own honest evaluation of our buried 'I've had it!' experiences.

I admit that until now I haven't even talked about my death urges with my family and friends, let alone with my colleagues. I mean, imagine in my current line of work where I'm running a new medical tech startup. After now admitting what I've gone through, will my partners question whether I can lead our team? Will they see me as being strong and brave for confessing what I just did in this chapter, will they still trust me to lead our team?

I suspect there are thousands of team leaders, maybe even millions of leaders, secretly asking themselves this same question. I'm currently an entrepreneur, a co-founder, a CEO with investors to consider – and I'm a woman with three kids immersed in a big family. They depend on me to be strong mentally and physically, to be a non-stop workhorse who's able to weather through any emotional or physical challenge.

But like everyone else, I also have my weaknesses, my times of hopelessness, and my occasional need for support rather than always being the supporter. I suspect that a great many of us are in similar situations where we know we're only human and can slip temporarily into utter despair – but our society doesn't support us in being honest, in openly seeking help, in temporarily breaking down and then hopefully emerging stronger than before.

I do hope we can change all this. Both genetically and from childhood conditioning, we all have particular dents in our personalities that we have to deal with and overcome – things we push away until they get under such immense inner pressure that they threaten to blow us up. But if we're able to express them and overcome them, we can gain greater perspective and strength. We might feel like bruised apples that have fallen many times and gotten a bit mushy in places – but we're both humbly and proudly still around!

From my business-leader perspective, all these tough-to-handle inner experiences have allowed me to grow and develop an inner strength so that I can now deal with the many challenges of bringing in funding and building a medical-device company. I've learned. I've matured. And I now know myself well enough to know I can take on and carry to fruition any responsibilities I agree to in business.

Perhaps most importantly, through my various suicide encounters I now know what to do if I become depressed again – first of all be honest with myself, then quickly reach out for help and speak honestly, as I have here. Accept that I'm fully human, and then deal with whatever comes my way. I'm a survivor, and hopefully I'm also able to offer support when others get down.

I can openly say now without hesitation – those bouts of extreme depression totally changed my whole life for the better. It's like a rebirth experience, a healing of who knows what. I'm sure for instance that my adult bouts of depression carried undertones tinged with extreme desperate feelings from my early childhood, and also from my parents' own childhood experiences and all the rest. We must accept the reality of our past.

By accepting and surviving, by facing and moving through the depths of agonizing despair, I now have a deeper appreciation of what it means to be human. I have an expanded new outlook that has emerged as a consequence of life traumas. I hope that everyone has the opportunity to move through their own unique experiences that offer this wake-up feeling. But I also hope that it's not necessary to go to such depths in order to rise up and embrace new strength and hope.

Chapter Twenty-Four

Having said all that, I want to end this book where it started – on the challenge all families must face to survive and thrive, to sustain themselves in a safe nurturing environment. At least here in America, aside from the native populations we're all immigrants. And a great many of us fled urgently to America like my family did, in order to escape a quite dire situation back home. So we all share the same basic story of being uprooted and then trying to sink new roots elsewhere.

The related theme of trying to raise one's children in a foreign country and culture resonates throughout my extended family and so many other families in America and elsewhere. The parents themselves are in shock from being uprooted, often traumatically – but at the same time they must do their very best to help their children adapt and assimilate and comprehend the new culture as fast as they can.

Certainly the leap from traditional Vietnam to modern-day America was gigantic for my parents. They tried to provide us with a sense of security and identity by maintaining the cultural norms they themselves had grown up within. But at the same time, they knew they had to do their best to prepare us to insert ourselves into an utterly different world.

This challenge is of course extra hard for refugees, because by definition they're not only from a foreign culture but they're also in rebellion against or otherwise fleeing a violent culture back home. I now have more compassion for when my dad would explode because of something I was doing that violated his beliefs, his culture, his prejudices and intentions.

As mentioned earlier, my dad became very angry with me when I went off to work in Thailand for a summer doing research. He blew up at me and refused to speak to me for months on end. Also when I decided not to go for my PhD, and instead took a trip to Vietnam, he hit the roof. And the third time I remember was when I decided to live together with Ark before marriage, to save money and be together as a couple. I tried but failed to help him see the situation beyond his traditional perspective.

I guess being the first child in a family is always a challenging stance. Obviously we don't choose to be the first-born. Also we don't choose our personality and who we are as an individual, even if it's radically different from everyone else. My strong convictions and 'do what feels right for me' persona often go against social, familial, and cultural norms. And our parents don't yet know how to parent – so the first child always has a fairly rough upbringing compared with the next siblings who have more experienced parents. With the younger children, my dad was beyond the Vietnamese traumas, he had gained some experience with the American culture, and was therefore much more lenient and understanding with them.

And for me as a mother, as I've shown earlier, my first-born daughter Leah was born into an environment that was chaotic and often traumatic both health-wise and emotionally. Even though I had been mostly raised in America and at least somewhat understood the new culture, I also like my parents wanted to preserve my family's culture and heritage.

I admit I didn't do a very good job at reconciling the two opposites of Vietnam and America. I ended up raising Leah in a quite privileged environment – but I also wanted her to feel her root identity as a refugee. I didn't see how wrong that approach was until many years later, and by then a lot of conflicting emotions and attitudes had developed between us.

Also – like my parents I approached parenting like a task. They worked non-stop year after year just to feed and house their children, and even as a very young child I also was under stress, doing everything I could in our household to help ease the strain of my parents. When times are tough families must stay tough emotionally – and I admit I perpetuated that warrior-gear armored-heart approach to life long after the extreme trauma was a thing of the past. Like my parents I ran my household on a tight schedule of things to get through each rushed day. I hugged Leah and kissed her as a baby, I wasn't cold. But my tendency was to carry on like my parents had, staying strong by keeping my distance when it came to feelings of the heart. I showed my love through doing everything, anything for Leah – but again like my parents, the words 'I love you' would never come out.

Looking back, I see that Leah tried to reach out to me in many ways, but I just never saw it. When she struggled in her own ways with the new problems of her generation, I never quite felt that they were real struggles – after all, she had a lovely home, she was living a totally privileged childhood compared with what I'd lived through. So I'd say, "Hey, you're living in America, you have plenty of food, you're safe and secure, you have all sorts of opportunities all around you. Stop complaining – you're fine."

And of course she hated that. She also hated that I'd drop everything, including spending time with her, when other people were struggling and needed my help – either their marriage was falling apart or they were depressed and suicidal or whatever. I would spend hours with others … and not with her. Recently I went for a social drink with a couple of neighbors and Leah pointed out that I found time for them but not for her. And she's right – I habitually leap to help people in need, and often in the process ignore the more subtle needs of my own kids.

And like my parents before me, it's still hard for me to understand and respond to the struggles of the new generation of more-privileged kids. It's obviously not their fault that they were born into the relative prosperity of the United States as opposed to the muddy bank of a Vietnamese river. Why do I still carry this weird attitude about keeping the raw refugee-survivor spirit alive in the hearts of children who have no memory or appreciation of where they've come from? I feel caught right between my parents' world and my children's world. So does Arkady.

Why do I feel guilty when I ease up and try to let my children fully embrace this new American reality that they're thankfully an integral part of? And how can I myself be true to where I came from, and at the same time also feel part of this new world? How can I finally let go of the gnawing feeling that I don't really belong here, that I'm an impostor who's suddenly going to be found out and kicked out?

One evening, my mentor for my new startup yelled at me and made me cry – but he was right. He told me I needed to own up to my position. He said I was acting so self-deprecating all the time, still caught up in feelings of not belonging – but maintaining that low-esteem stance was not at all helpful if I wanted to successfully lead a company. I heard him, and his words hurt because they were so true.

But it's such a great challenge to somehow let go and move on into the new, when so much of my identity is still caught up in the attitudes and struggles of a long-gone past. I recently needed to do an assignment for a business presentation, writing something about who I am as CEO of my company, expressing why I'm the best person to lead this company. I know I'm fully able to lead the company to success, but it was very difficult to express that in sincere authentic words.

It's not that I lack confidence in doing the work. It's just that, as you've seen from my life story, my identity was set before I went to college – and that identity will always feel out of place in this privileged world I've advanced step by step into. How many immigrants feel that same way: "Do I deserve to be here?" That's probably why I don't sleep enough, why I'm constantly overextending myself trying to make sure everything's perfect. I'm still trying to demonstrate my self-worth, unable to sit still because there's always too much to get done.

My ingrained attitude is that I can't just enjoy being a housewife. That would be too privileged a life role for someone like me – after all, a refugee mother cannot be just a housewife. My own mom worked so hard earning money and running her household at the same time – so I must also. A friend recently told me outright to stop killing myself by overworking like I do. My husband's business is thriving, we don't really need additional money. And he's right – why am I killing myself by building these startups?

The answer that comes to my mind is that I don't feel like my work out in the world is done. My nature or my programming, or both, is to work work work – and yes, I do fully enjoy working! I still don't quite know what I'm pursuing, but it's very satisfying to create new businesses with services or products that I feel are genuinely needed. And I thoroughly enjoy taking risks, just like my dad did.

Last week I had the opportunity to speak to sixth-graders in Washington, D.C. about my refugee story. I gave a simple talk over Zoom, but I was very nervous for some reason. I stumbled through my talk, but the students seemed to be quite interested. I had a ton of questions from them, and one of the questions really struck me: "Did you have a special passion when you were my age?" My response came out of my mouth before I could reflect on whether it was appropriate for this class: "No, I didn't – because passion is for the privileged."

Afterward, I reflected on the idea that if I'd had the opportunity as a child to indulge in a passion for something, I would have explored many new things – but I had received zero opportunity or encouragement to explore my youthful passions. And I realized that one of the reasons I get upset with my kids when they show no interest in opportunities I offer them, is because I never had the possibility to follow my passions and learn new things, at least not until I got to college.

To be honest, until around puberty I don't think I even knew what passion was. But then when my English teacher introduced me to reading novels for the first time, and I read that *Jane Eyre* book, I started for the first time to develop a passion for something – a deep feeling of excitement and hunger to learn new things, to explore new experiences, to feel new feelings. And that passion was what opened the doors that led me to attend college and venture into new realms.

Now I have many passions that move me to explore and create – some very simple, like finding beautiful little things to string together into a necklace for a friend. And I also harbor very large passions for getting ever deeper into science, and right now, building a med-tech company that's grounded totally in science. When my current startup opportunity appeared out of the blue, there was no question – I was passionate about doing it, and I'm now following that passion – despite no experience in the field.

My kids and I watched *Hamilton* together. Afterward they told me I'm just like Hamilton – whatever comes my way, I'm going to do it, even at the detriment of my family and friends. And yes, that's me. Some people think I'm selfish because I'm so tightly focused on certain things. I'm not the idealized mom catering to her kids and doing what they want all the time. And I'm finally learning not to feel guilty for who I am.

Like I mentioned earlier, when people view someone from the outside they reflexively create their own story about that person's life, inner feelings and intentions – assumptions that often don't match reality at all. Who can say what pushes someone to make certain choices and then act on them? What past experiences, dreams and traumas have shaped them, molded their personalities and pushed them into expressing their present attitudes and actions?

I often stop in at a local coffee shop that I really like. The owner makes amazing coffee but you can't ask him to deviate from his preferred approach – you can't ask him for fake sugar or non-diary creamer or anything like that. You can't even ask for low fat milk. You just get what he gives you, because he thinks coffee should be done in a particular optimum way.

The owner yells at customers a lot. He yelled at me last week. He usually doesn't yell at me, but when I went in that morning to buy my son a muffin, I didn't have enough cash, and the owner doesn't take credit cards below a certain dollar amount – so I ordered a coffee and walked out. I came back after dropping my son off and got hollered at for that. Earlier in my life I would have hollered back in defense, or stomped out and never returned. But instead of reacting, I didn't say anything. Then I quietly said I was sorry.

The reason I don't get upset by those situations anymore is because I recognize that I don't know what has happened in his life, what caused him to be this way. And that realization saves me a lot of conflict with people – and I like that. The man after all has a passion for making coffee, and I also found out that he used to be a public defender, which means he probably has a big heart under all his bluster – but most people don't know that, so his hollering puts them off.

Perhaps that's the whole point of this story. You've come to understand my history, so you can perhaps accept the choices I make in my life, or perhaps don't make, and grant me the space and freedom to be who I am. And I'll do my best to do the same with you if we ever meet. This seems to be the basis for a harmonious community – everyone realizing we're all just the end sum of our whole life experience. It seems that continuous unconditional kindness, like in my father's Buddhist and my mom's Catholic upbringing, is probably the greatest virtue for all of us to aspire toward.

If there's a rule or lesson or a guideline here, it's a request that we stop habitually judging the people around us just by their seemingly-crazy actions. We don't know what they've come through to make them behave as they do now. And if we want people to be patient and understanding with us, we do need to do the same for them. I think every culture and tradition in the world holds this golden rule as primary to a good life and a sustainable culture.

Ending Thoughts

~~~~~~~~~~~~~~~~~~~~~~~~~~~~

My life is now so very different from where it started on the banks of the Mekong. I have had the fortune to experience everything from sitting chilled and hungry in abject poverty to sitting at dinner tables surrounded by individuals dripping in extreme wealth. I have felt love and pain. I have succeeded and failed. I now live in the very place that I once thought was snooty, returning to Ark's childhood town of Brookline to raise our kids. I have been discriminated against, only to later be loved by that same discriminator.

I'm so fortunate to have experienced both ends and everything in the middle of the socio-economic totem pole. I'm so thankful that somehow I've managed to become somewhat tolerant to people who are worlds apart from me at many levels. There have been many times when I was culturally myopic and intolerant. But I also had many experiences where I was taught to let go of prejudices and embrace people very different from myself. Hopefully we're all learning how to be more kind, both to others and to ourselves.

Our whole world seems to be currently drowning in antagonistic self-righteous views, with so many people never lending an ear to hear or accept anything that's even remotely different from their own programmed attitudes and beliefs. When people can't open
~~~~~~~~~~~~~~~~~~~~~~~~~~~~

up to respect and support the views of anyone outside their circle of fellow believers, their culture is truly in danger.

How can we learn to accept others who are worlds apart from us? How can we solve all our deeper problems, even locally at home, if we don't open up our minds and hearts? My Russian in-laws for instance, as I have narrated in my story, didn't want their son to marry a non-Russian non-Jew and propagate yellow grandchildren. But then over time, through the sharing of my Vietnamese world with them and embracing their world, we've all come to feel family together – we no longer feel worlds apart.

I'm so very thankful that my family has evolved from our war-torn destitute beginnings in Vietnam to our current abundant and peaceful life here in America. But despite our fortunate life situation, there are still times when the dark clouds suddenly overwhelm me. My situation is now vastly different compared to half-starving in a dangerous war-smashed part of the world. But still, even in America, almost everyone seems to occasionally get overwhelmed with feelings of anxiety and depression. Inner cycles repeat themselves even as we evolve into a hopefully better future.

What am I saying here? Perhaps that life remains a challenging mystery – it's at heart totally inexplicable. What we and our ancestors experienced in the past does continue to influence our experience in the present moment. And this means that every time we interact with someone, we need to remember that we're interacting with the entirety of that person's heritage. They might be worlds apart from us culturally, but we share this core experience of being heartfully human – and that realization will bond us together!

When I close my eyes, sometimes a memory or feeling pops into my mind that triggers a memory or feeling from the past. Who knows what part of who I've been is rising to the surface. Often tears will come streaming down my cheeks as I get temporarily caught up in something beyond my current mundane situation. I now do my best not to push those feelings away. Instead I try to stay open and fully embrace what's rising up – and I hopefully allow some much-needed healing to happen.

When I'm willing to do this, especially to face my past demons, I can then say okay, that's over and done with, it's time to let go and move on. It seems that only when I manage to accept, forgive, and let go of the past, am I able to relax … and feel free and fulfilled in the present moment.

All while I was growing up and struggling with the various challenges we've explored in this book, I never dared to imagine having this remarkable American life I've ended up with – a wonderful loving husband, great kids who drive me insane, amazing opportunities to explore and a wealth of friendships. But here I am! And whenever a glimmer of the past comes hauntingly to mind, returning me right back to the banks of the Mekong, I feel spontaneously thankful for the sometimes-turbulent flow of my life thus far – and I feel hope rising up that a great many other people can be similarly blessed with peace, abundance, and the healing touch of human kindness.

One thing is for sure – my journey has allowed me to explore myself as a full person, to mature and discover what's most important in life. And I know I wouldn't have gotten here if I hadn't been surrounded by so many people who have elevated my spirit and offered me a chance to create a life that's not worlds apart from my neighbor.

Goodbye Paris!

As a final uplifting note, I'd like to end with this short account of what happened right after finishing the layout and final editing of *Worlds Apart*. Eagerly and rather impulsively I booked a flight to Paris. Those solitary experiences I mentioned earlier, sitting quietly on benches in Paris, had been so transformational many years ago. The City of Lights had served as my mental rock whenever shit hit the fan in my life. So after wrapping up the book, I sought out Paris once again to help me recenter, decompress, and take time to re-discover my inner sense of freedom.

However, unlike previous times, I didn't go to Paris alone. Instead I brought my daughter along with me, to give her an opportunity to see me in my elements, and more importantly to give us a fresh opportunity to rebuild 14 years of an uneven relationship. That mother-daughter part of the trip to Paris evolved beautifully – but my current relationship with Paris itself was unexpectedly a bit of a surprise.

Upon landing in Paris one Friday morning in late July 2021 and driving from Charles de Gaulle Airport to Paris Rive Droite in the 16th arrondissement, I found that I somehow wasn't feeling any excitement or arousal as I entered the city. That bright liberating sense of *je ne sais quoi* was missing and for the first time ever, I felt completely indifferent to Paris. Perhaps I was just tired, I told myself. After all, I'd barely slept the previous week while wrapping up as much work as possible and preparing my family to be without me for a week.

During the next several days my daughter and I wandered through many miles of the city, from the 16th to the 4th arrondissements, along the Seine and into some quite ethnic local communities that remain unexplored by most tourists. We sat in cafés sipping perfectly-crafted cappuccinos surrounded by gargoyle details of gothic architectural buildings. I again watched the local Parisians going about their daily routines. We sat on benches and relaxed into the quite agreeable foreign vibes, and walked the city with no goals in mind. Peaceful, relaxing. But still … I felt nothing compared to my previous more-intense visits.

I realized toward the end of our week in France that I still enjoyed Paris – but no longer needed it. All I needed in order to feel content and uplifted was being with my daughter. For the first time since I could remember, I held her hand walking back from dinner one night. And spontaneously during another dinner, we embraced each other, which rarely happens. This time in Paris, closeness with her was what I needed – and I felt so thankful simply to feel us both opening up to newness in our relationship.

Paris had indeed transformed me in earlier years. As some sort of ephemeral embracing presence the city had always been there for me, giving me more than I could ever give back. That city will always be in my heart and always be special – but I can now close my chapter on Paris. Au revoir, mon amour!

During that flight home I realized that for the first time ever, I have opened up to a deep feeling that I was always afraid of. For the longest time I allowed the negative aspects of being a refugee to inhibit me from expressing my full spontaneous enjoyment of life. I've always held up a lifelong refugee-badge as my excuse for all of my negativities. Now as I return home from Paris, I feel that I can let all of that go. I'll always be a refugee, my past has obviously forever shaped me – but it doesn't have to continue to define me.

My first time in Paris, I spontaneously discovered myself. This time, as I'm leaving Paris I'm also leaving behind my refugee past. Now I'm just me.

Mai Kim Le

Questions To Ponder

~~~~~~~~~~~~~~~~~~~~~~~~

Both on your own, and perhaps in a reading group or class discussion, you might find the following questions of value for eliciting expanded conversations and insights on a number of themes touched upon in this book:

Q 1: Except for indigenous populations, America is made up entirely of immigrants. How do you see yourself in this light?

Q 2: The author has taken the risk of being bluntly honest in her narration. Do you think it's a good idea to be so forthcoming about one's life, or did the author go too far in her personal revelations?

Q 3: The author also has been true to her particular upbringing and attitudes rather than making this story entirely politically correct. Did you admire her honesty, or should her story have been edited to be politically correct?

Q 4: All too often, families tend to romanticize their immigration accounts as the generations go by. Does your family still tell true stories of your ancestral journey to America or wherever they ended up? And are these stories solidly based on fact, or have they become embellished and romanticized?

Q 5: Being a refugee is different from being an immigrant – in that a refugee is actively fleeing a dangerous situation back home, whereas an immigrant is usually acting more out of hope for the future than fear of a present situation. What's' your identity in this regard?
~~~~~~~~~~~~~~~~~~~~~~~~

Q 6: Mai does her best to recall and express her raw feelings from her past – but she doesn't dwell overmuch on the suffering she experiences. Would you have liked more detail, or was the balance just right?

Q 7: Mai's story is an extreme account – ranging from her infancy of absolute destitution in Vietnam to studying at Princeton University twenty years later. Why was she able to accomplish what she did?

Q 8: The love story of this narration is unique, portraying two children of refugee and immigrant parents who were worlds apart in heritage, but who managed to bridge that ancestral gap with love. What do you think of friendships and marriages that manage to merge different cultures into a new sense of family?

Q 9: The underlying immigrant issue of mental health and especially depression and PTSD arises often in Mai's story of her life. What are your feelings about mental health– do you have any fresh ideas about how America might be of more help to all those who're struggling?

Q 10: Food is also central to this account. Mai began her life half-starving, experienced bulimia in college – but then ended up a great cook who loves preparing feasts for family and friends. Does food play a central role in your own family life?

Q 11: As immigrants sink roots and find some success and upward mobility in their new homeland, they must deal with their changing attitudes toward more recent immigrants. Each new generation struggles to move ahead without losing the importance of their family traditions. How has your family dealt with this challenge – does cultural assimilation necessarily have to mean loss of ancestral identity?

Q 12: Dialect and local identity is important in Mai's account. She felt actually more at home in her early rough teen neighborhoods than later on in more well-to-do neighborhoods. What did you think about her struggles in this regard – and do you feel you've forever left behind your own family's early roots and dialects?

Q 13: Mai has openly shared her experience in order to help break free from the barriers of silence in the Asian American community. Do you think that in violating these cultural inhibitions she is helping or hurting the community? And what might she have said or done differently?

Q 14: Mai makes many analogies to western-culture films, philosophers, artists and so forth throughout the book. Do you find such Eurocentric analogies helpful, or antithetical to her experience as a refugee?

Q 15: It's often said that failure in various ways is necessary for growth and ultimate success. Mai failed in many ways – and often times more than once, twice, and thrice before succeeding. At what point should one just accept failure, quit and move on?

Q 16: In *Worlds Apart*, Mai struggles through an often-painful and difficult love relationship that requires patience and forgiveness many times over. Would you have walked away after the first, second, third, or forth marriage fiasco if you'd been in her shoes? When is enough enough? And – are such deep relationship between people of different cultural or economic background a good idea, or to be avoided?

Special Thanks

~~~~~~~~~~~~~~~~~~~~~~~~~~

My resolution every New Year has been to write this book – but my over-busy life kept pushing my dream of writing to the back burner. Then my happenchance encounter with John Selby, a noted psychologist and author coach, finally enabled me to realize my literary dream. Without John I wouldn't have been able to accomplish this goal – thank you, John, for being by my side through this process, allowing me to speak my mind without inhibition, and helping me mold my raw outflow into beautiful prose.

I wouldn't have been able to string together the Vietnam escape story without making my parents relive their hardest memories. They knew how important writing this book was to me, and they broke over 40 years of silence to provide the details of the escape. I provoked tears and pain that I wish I hadn't, but I hope that remembering those experiences has helped them heal and put the past behind them.

Writing is one the hardest thing for me. When speaking from my heart, the pages of this book sometimes emerged rather easily. But usually, with a tight work schedule and demands of family, I often had to resort to all-nighters and weekend writing marathons to complete this book. On many fronts I would never have made it through this process without my pillar and dearest love, my husband – who provided essential emotional support throughout this creative endeavor.

Enduring friendships are my chosen family. My three closest Pakistani friends, Mehvesh, Naeem, and Hasnain, lent me their eyes and hearts as they read different excerpts I'd written about
~~~~~~~~~~~~~~~~~~~~~~~~~~

our shared past. *Shukriya* to all three of you for your unconditional support and love.

This book entailed a lot of challenging self-reflection that surfaced during a number of years. This movement toward self-realization was made possible through the help of my therapist, Frances, who listened without labels or judgement and enabled me to identify my problems and find solutions in order to grow and heal. Thank you, Frances, for listening and relistening all these years.

To my other dear friends – Alex, Fan, Tara, Meenakshi, Julie, Diana, Reni, Lisa, David, Loan, Shelly, Reggie, Rodney, Irene, John, KG, Carla, and many others who stuck with me through this process even in the hardest moments – thank you for your friendship, love, and support. More importantly, thank you for taking the time out of your busy schedules to read the manuscript and provide valuable feedback.

As hard as this book was and still is for my own family, thank you for working through the challenges of this book and ultimately supporting me regardless of how challenging the story is in your hearts and minds, I truly believe we will grow stronger together and work towards fully healing our past. I love you three very much.

My dearest cousins from Washington, how would I have been able to get through the tough times of this book (and life in general) without your understanding and support. I cried so often while completing the manuscript, and you were there at all hours to talk to me. That's true family!

My boatmate, Minnie, thank you for listening and helping me through the toughest part of this journey. Our shared experiences have kept us close. Love you!

I always thought it was frivolous to spend money on art, feeling that art is a privilege and treasure that should be made available to the world regardless of one's socioeconomic background.

While growing up I simply didn't understand art. But after my studies in Paris I fell in love with all forms of art, gaining a greater understanding of the power of colors, shapes, and strokes to evoke an experience that's often more powerful than words. After Paris I was often in search of Vietnamese art that spoke to me – and then I discovered Ha Duong of Ha Ha Art from Hoi An. Recently I was able to procure his provocative and stunning art piece that graces the cover of this book and website. Please support our artists wherever possible, and follow Ha on Instagram @haduongart and at https://haduongart.com.

In writing this book, I met so many great people who have helped me along the way. I thank all of you, from the bottom of my heart, who helped with different aspects of this project: Birgitta, Jesse, Hasan, Feeza, Joe, and Waterside Publishing. And also many thanks to my team at Haystack Dx for your understanding and support of this project during an intense development process.

It surely takes a village to write a book!

~~~~~~~~~~~~~~~~~~~~~
~~~~~~~~~~~~~~~~~~~~~

Please feel free to join me for open discussions of many of the shared themes I explored in Worlds Apart at any of the following social media platforms:

My Website: www.maikimle.com

Facebook: @mai.unplugged

Twitter & Instagram: @mai_unplugged

~~~~~~~~~~~~~~~~~~~~~~~~~~~~~~~~~~~~
~~~~~~~~~~~~~~~~~~~~~~~~~~~~~~~~~~~~

Made in United States
North Haven, CT
19 October 2021